Millennium

Discourse on humanity, human nature, human consciousness, the human narrative, and the human condition

Sentience changed everything...

by Whickwithy

Humanity was meant for better than this. Our future depends on clarity of awareness.

"Education of the mind without education of the heart is no education at all."
   -Aristotle

Millennium

All rights reserved

ISBN: 978-1-7348221-1-3

Millennium by Whickwithy

First published in early 2021
Refined in November 2021
Final Edition Mid November 2022
Revised March 2023

Previous publications on the same subject:
Sentience
A Sentient Perspective
Beauty & Fiction

"The smell of a world that is burned"
   - Jimi Hendrix

"Power at its most vicious is a riposte to powerlessness."
   - Simone de Beauvoir

"When will our consciences grow so tender that we will act to prevent human misery rather than avenge it?"
   - Eleanor Roosevelt

"Sure he (Fred Astaire) was great, but don't forget that Ginger Rogers did everything he did, ...backwards and in high heels."
   - Bob Thaves, "Frank and Ernest" comic strip

"Darkness cannot drive out darkness; only light can do that. Hate cannot drive out hate; only love can do that."
   - Martin Luther King, Jr.

"And nothing natural is evil"
   -Marcus Aurelius

"The unexamined life is not worth living"
"Let he that would move the world first move himself"
"From the deepest desires often come the deadliest hate"
   - Socrates

"History is a pack of lies about events that never happened told by people who weren't there."
   - George Santayana

"The reason why the world lacks unity, and lies broken and in heaps, is, because man is disunited with himself."
   -Ralph Waldo Emerson

"What lies behind you and what lies in front of you, pales in comparison to what lies inside of you."
   -Ralph Waldo Emerson

"And that's the thing
Do you recognize the bell of truth
When you hear it ring"
    -Leon Russell

"For truth is always strange; stranger than fiction."
    -Lord Byron

"I've got some words to say about the way we live today.
Why can't we learn to love each other.
It's time to learn a new face for the whole world wide human race."
    -Leon Russell

"We are what we repeatedly do. Therefore, excellence is not an act, but a habit."
    -Aristotle

**"A little learning is a dangerous thing
Drink deep, or taste not the Pierian Spring"**
    -Alexander Pope

"There are only two ways to live your life. One is as though nothing is a miracle. The other is as though everything is a miracle."
    - Albert Einstein

"Violence is the last refuge of the incompetent."
    -Isaac Asimov

"It is never too late to be what you might have been."
    - George Eliot

"We accept the love we think we deserve."
    - Stephen Chbosky

"I saw ten thousand talkers whose tongues were all broken"
    -Bob Dylan

"One who asks a question feels like a fool for a moment. One who refuses to ask a question feels a fool for a lifetime." Or, a sentient race remains a fool for millennia.
    -Japanese proverb

Humanity remains a dilettante at sentience, a poser. We're on the threshold of something more, something human.

Table of contents

Liberation of the heart

Aristotle said, "Education of the mind without education of the heart is no education at all."

In the three thousand years since that statement was made we have *never* educated the heart.

Eleanor Roosevelt queried, ""When will our consciences grow so tender that we will act to *prevent* human misery rather than avenge it?"

When we become human. When we educate the heart, accept our sentient state, and unleash our humanity.

Unlike intelligence, education of the heart is not a matter of learning from books.

Besides intelligence, there is a much more significant sentient trait that has been all but overlooked. Awareness. Our awareness, just like our intelligence, is far more developed than an animal, yet we have not applied it.

Welcome to the next level of the game of life. It's called human awareness. So far, we have only utilized our intelligence. That was the easy part. Once we unleash our awareness, we will finally unleash our heart and our humanity. Our emotional state will become stable and the heart will have been educated.

We avoid our awareness. In three thousand years, humanity itself has not changed one iota. There lies our biggest problem.

Picking away at each individual problem, like, climate change (as horrible as it is and, yes, it still needs to be addressed), endless wars with meaningless justification, misogyny, inequality and inequitable treatment of so many, *especially* women, is not enough. You can legislate until you are blue in the face, and nothing changes until you seek the source of *all* of these issues. What makes humanity so dystopian? I guarantee you, the answer will surprise you.

It is not enough to expose our problems by whining about them. We know what they are. Wee try to suppress the issues through laws and such. We complain ad nauseam but never do anything of import to *eliminate* the problems.

We shout "love is good" and "war is bad". It never changes a thing. We just look on as the juggernaut of our past continues to run us down.

Attempting to force people (e.g. laws, peer pressure, religion, etc) to act a certain way is infantile. It is Pavlov's dog. It is an animal's answer to a sentient question that has never been asked: What is wrong with humanity?

The question we have to be asking ourselves is why are we such a dysfunctional race and what can be done about it? Worse yet, somewhere along the line, we convinced ourselves that we are irreparably damaged. So, we throw up our hands and whine.

We have only needed to step back and see the big picture. We have to admit that there is something wrong at a very fundamental level. The level of humanity.

There is something wrong with humanity itself. There is grit in the machine that causes dysfunction of a sentient race. Something remains from our animal legacy that does not suit a sentient race. Our sentient awareness has always sensed this.

The answer, when you look deeply enough, is no, we do not need to remain the horrifying race of inept, supposedly sentient beings that we currently portray. It has all been an act.

We need to educate the heart and it is easily done.

The big picture

Try to look back to the point in time when humanity first realized it was different from the other animals, when it tried to grasp its increased intellect *and* awareness. What went wrong? Why did we go so crazy? Our sentient awareness was subjugated because our ancient ancestors became bewildered.

We could not accept one specific realization that our sentient awareness developed. It blasted our minds. That broke our sentience as we continued to hide from the most important realization that would change humanity into something far more than any animal. Something human. Something loving. Something beautiful. No utopia but not an unadulterated dystopian mess.

Premise

How does a self-aware race treat women equitably while coitus, the foundation of human, *sentient* existence and the forge on which the most important human relationship, the one in which procreation is wrought, remains inequitable (i.e. a *sentient* failure), an inept animal's act?

All of humanity's troubles stem from this situation, *not* answering this question. We have never even been *aware* of the issue. It befuddled our ancient ancestors to such an extent, they suppressed the issue thoroughly.

I really, really can't explain humanity's dilemma regarding sentience any better than that. It is the core issue that has always faced humanity and *never* faced any previous animal. For a billion years, the animal's version of coitus was incomplete. Why should we think it could change, should change?

We haven't really faced the issue yet. Thus, it has ripped us apart. We remain an animal until we face this issue and coitus becomes human.

There has never been a more fundamental, crucial, dismaying problem facing humanity. Without answering this question, as a race of sentient beings, we will continue to face aggravation, frustration, misery, and failure. The relationship between man and woman will remain a shambles until it is addressed.

The current answer is to avoid the question altogether. That has led to humanity becoming insane and utterly destructive.

The wrong answer is to create a pill to substitute for manhood.

The broken answer, well, there are a lot of broken answers, all on display.

The easy answer is every man accepting that it is their responsibility to make the sexual experience equitable for the woman (e.g. dildo, cunnilingus, etc). That would improve our situation drastically. Any way in which two people achieve mutual pleasure is better than not. It is not, however, a completely sentient answer. At best, it is a stopgap that may very well continue to have its place.

The sentient answer is men naturally improving their performance at unassisted coitus to the point that they can love a woman eye-to-eye. That doesn't exclude other ways in which two people achieve pleasure. But, accepting that coitus is excluded from attaining mutual pleasure is not sentient.

In other words, until we take seriously a sentient perspective on the issue of men's unassisted coital performance, coitus will remain wanting and so will humanity. Many men will remain an insane, demented, animal haunted by their failure and many women will remain a shadow of themselves.

There is no doubt that men can improve their performance at coitus. We are sentient.

I detail the factors that lead to improving any man's performance to the point that they achieve loving coitus later in this book. It is thorough, yet it is still only the beginning.

Everything I have previously written on the subject was the necessary exploration of the baffling, miserable human condition and its source. Articulating that the complex, suppressed issue regarding our welfare as a sentient race has not be easy. How does a sentient race treat women equitably while coitus, the driving factor for human existence and the basis for the most important human relationship, remains inequitable? Or, how does a sentient race treat women equitably without equitable sexual relations? Or, how does a race of sentient potential become one with its sentience?

The hidden depths behind that question are formidable. How does a man love himself if he cannot love another? How does humanity become human while suppressing the issue which can finally make it human.

Everyone seeks their own peace of mind amidst a situation that overturns the sanity of the race or howls for pointless change that means absolutely nothing if we do not first become human in every sense of the word.

I don't believe anyone is stupid but the vast majority (like everybody) is stupoured, *unaware*. We have been forced into a state of stupour by the nonsense that filled the gap in place of an answer to that all-important question, that overriding situation. Everything, *everything* has developed in accordance with avoiding that question.

All that I have previously written provides the details: the history of our befuddlement, the false trails we have followed, as well as the traps we have set for ourselves.

My apologies for not having all the answers in the first three books. Worse yet, I fumbled the telling of the tale of our inability to rise above the animal and proclaim our sentient state. It is an extremely difficult tale to tell when everyone has their own prejudices predetermined by the conditioning they have endured all their lives. First, by the childhood brainwashing of the culture in which they were raised that is embellished further by the delusions they create for themselves post-pubescence.

As you can imagine, it has been an arduous journey to identify all of the paradigms of nonsense that have built up over the last three millennia and overcome those that were specifically attached to myself. The previous three books were my first attempts to peer through the bewilderment, confusion, and outright deceits that led us by the nose, thus producing three millennia of agony.

Maybe the most extraordinary realization is that the male gender has been running a bluff since the beginning of our existence as a highly aware race. Our heightened awareness has always known better. Whether we wanted to accept that awareness or not, our sentience was relentless. It has always known that we were meant for better.

The bluff has been the ultimate irony. The bluff has wrecked our sentient existence for many millennia. Finally, after all of the pain and suffering, it will become the truth that makes us human. In other words, the bluff was never a bluff. It's just that no one realized it. Until now.

Synopsis

What does it mean to be human? There are, currently, two general schools of thought. Both sell us short.

One view is that being human doesn't really mean much or matter much. We are just a smarter animal and should expect to act like one. All of the ruthlessness should be expected. One should join in the fun. Sometimes, it is referred to, sadly, as "the animal spirit" or suggested as proven in some way by Darwin's theory. They believe the existing, awful human condition that we have endured for millennia is as good as it gets. Existentialism is the be-all to end-all. Only the strong survive and all of the other niaiserie of the animal.

The second interpretation of being human is that we must keep our nose to the grindstone, never look up, and at some distant point in the far distant future (or, in some afterlife), we may wake up and find we are finally something more than an animal. "We have potential." Just *act* like we're human long enough, just say, "I think I can, I think I can!" and we'll get there, sooner or later. Keep that nose to the grindstone. We just need training. Like Pavlov's Dog.

The former thought process looks at the latter with scorn as if the latter were an animal putting on airs. The latter perceives the former as lost.

They are both wrong. They are both right. There is far more to the human race and we *don't* have to wait ages.

In fact, the question and the answer have always been buried amidst the flotsam of our most distant past. We just missed it. The topic itself existed for a billion years before humans.

We need to do some excavation.

Femininity, masculinity, & humanity

Funny thing, the female spirit. I adore it, right down to my bones.

What I began to wonder, though, is how much of what we consider feminine characteristics are, in actuality, the human part of a woman that both genders *should* share? There is something clearly missing in men. We consider them feminine characteristics because the human, sentient characteristics that women display have been mostly absent in the male.

We have been trapped in a nightmare of remaining an animal by a single stroke, but we can be human. We have all of the equipment gifted to us by an extraordinary evolution, far beyond the potential of animals. We're just not using the gifts well at all ... yet. Part of the issue is that we haven't realized that evolution *for a sentient race* is not just about the genes but using the gifts those genetic changes provided in a sentient manner.

There is so much more to humanity. Human nature far exceeds what our human conditions suggest. Human existence remains out of true, unfulfilled.

Human *nature* is represented by all of the most amazing qualities, like love, honour, integrity, etc that humanity defined long, long ago but has seldom attained, even in small measure. Those finer qualities exist in the *natural* state of the fully sentient human. They are not something to strive for. They are gifts that easily thrive in a sentient race, once the gifts are no longer trod upon by animals from the time we are born.

They are not goals. They are not something to attain, something to grasp for. They are inherent in a human. They are currently undermined in the most curious manner throughout each human's lifetime.

The human, sentient mind conceived of these many virtuous qualities long ago. Our current state cannot maintain them because the animal lingers. The finer qualities of our human nature seem to slip through our fingers like water.

Those finer human qualities are a *potential* with which we are born. We fritter them all away over a lifetime. The human *condition* does *not* reflect human *nature*. The human *condition* crushes all of the natural, finer sentient qualities right out of us.

We have convinced ourselves that all of the human chaos we endure is to be expected. It's all we've known. We have convinced ourselves that it is just the miserable lot of a sentient race. That is so wrong as to be offensive. "We are only human" may be the most despicable phrase ever created.

I will lay out the situation as it is and the method by which we become an emotionally stable, rational, loving race of sentient beings without all of the clamour and noise. After all this time, we can rid ourselves of the animal that lingers.

I'll create a new phrase, "Goodness! We are human!"

Sentience

Sentience is typically defined as extraordinarily heightened intellect and awareness. By that definition, it occurred for humanity many thousands of years ago.

Missing from this formal definition of sentience are curiosity, creativity, and imagination that develop alongside heightened awareness and intellect.

We have used those traits of imagination and creativity to convince ourselves that we are nothing more than a really smart animal. In essence, we have been hiding from a trait of the animal that we have not been able to shake loose and holds us back from attaining our sentience and those very appropriate finer qualities.

Our subjugated sentient awareness has always known there was something more to being human, whether we liked it or not, whether we could figure it out or not, whether we were willing to admit it or not.

We never pinned down those finer qualities well enough to make them a feature of being human.

Our curiosity led us to a realization that we were not ready to confront. We stumbled across a situation with which we couldn't cope so early during our emergence into sentience. Imagination and creativity kicked in to obscure the trait that our curiosity had uncovered. That was the first nail in the coffin of our sentience. It became a habit. Call that habit lying.

While we still knew next to nothing, we desperately sought answers, whether they made sense or not. In such a way, the most infamous phrase *ever* was created, "We're only human." It makes my skin crawl. *Only* human?!!?! That was the second nail in the coffin.

Some seem to believe that, if we keep striving, we will incrementally improve over centuries and millennia. How's that going for you? Do you see any substantial drop in violence, hate, insane reactions? Any drop at all? At best, the mania only becomes suppressed.   That does not get us any closer to becoming human.

Another definition of sentience (i.e. from the word "senses") is a more sophisticated ability to *feel* emotions.

Our emotional makeup went haywire long ago. "We're only human" seems to cover that well. It is such a perfect excuse for remaining animal. We might as well be saying, "we are only an animal." It is a lie.

We are an animal that was gifted but, in no way, knew what to do with our heightened intellect, what our heightened awareness forced us to confront regarding an animal's existence, or our emotions. We did somewhat better with the brains. The emotions and awareness remain a shambles. There's a reason for that.

This state of emotional upheaval is often mistaken for human nature rather than just the miserable conditions of a sentient being that has yet to attain its potential. A sentient being that remains, for all intents and purposes, an animal. A sentient being that remains in a stupour.

It is sometimes even suggested that our unstable emotions are at the heart of our problems (think Mr. Spock).   Out-of-control emotions are a symptom, not the disease. Emotions are not the problem. They are a gift. We just have to figure out why they are hair-trigger haywire.

Stable emotions are the nature of a fully developed sentient being. Hair-trigger emotional upheaval is humanity's *condition*, most apparent in men, *not* its *nature*.

It became clear long ago that there is a better way than rampaging around like a wounded animal. Love, and all of the finer qualities that humanity envisions, such as honour and integrity, honesty and dignity, were conceived long ago. Their essence becomes dislodged over a lifetime. Emotions fall apart and the finer qualities just drift away. Something is missing.

We came up with the excuse that "we're only human." That was the death knell that began the downward spiral of all of our aspirations to become something more than an animal. We, essentially, became an animal in really, really nice clothes, dressed up for the party that never occurred and uncomfortable in the accoutrements of sentience.

That trifling phrase and a few thousand years of confusion and defeat have replaced our high expectations. There is near complete acceptance of our dystopia and stupour. We act as if it were the result of our human nature rather than the simple expedient of our ongoing befuddlement regarding human nature and that which holds us back from attaining a loving existence.

Achieving our human nature is not a long drawn out process as it is portrayed. It has only been delayed by our own obfuscation. We have not attained the single missing element that allows us to maintain the stable sentient, human and humane outlook that coincides with human nature because we have avoided the all-important question.

As we fulfill our human nature, we will, simultaneously, rid ourselves of the last dregs of the animal.

There is barely a glimmer left of those finer qualities as we become resigned to being little more than an animal, just smarter. The vicious actions of the human animal speak for themselves.

Some have concluded that intellect and knowledge are what *caused* all of our trouble. Original sin and all that. That there is nothing to be done about it. They'd rather return to the animal state of stupour. We might as well curl up in a ball and wait for death. *Then*, it will get better.

It is not knowledge but lack of comprehension of our situation that has doomed us. We have taken detours and become mesmerized by the distractions that we throw in the way of clarity, up until now. We are not too fond of looking in the mirror of our humanity. We obscured the truth because it confounded us. What a grave mistake that was.

The goal of those finer qualities that we so desire represent the attainment of a sane existence that matches our human nature. The terms themselves are our fumbling attempts to define that which we sense in youth and throw away as we (as a race as well as individuals) become discouraged.

Humanity has an extremely strong desire for love, compassion, honour, integrity, honesty, physical bonding and clarity.   We sense them all early in life.   It begins to get drummed out of us from the moment we are born and becomes cemented six feet under in our teens and twenties as we transition into our post-pubescent state.   Yet, we still have an intuitive sense that humanity should behave in a loving, compassionate manner.

Something ruthlessly crushes every attempt at achieving a noble, respectable existence under the boot.   Something chains us to an animal's perspective, one generation after another, driving the human race to despair and rampage, like a wounded animal, as each generation throws its hope in the gutter.

The easy, lazy answer is "we're only human", so just put up with it.   It'll get better *after* you die (??!?!).   The more difficult answer is that we're missing a bet.

Something consistently drives us back to the dumbfounded state of an animal.   The twisted trail of delusions we have left in our wake makes it almost impossible to ascertain what is wrong.

Something blocks the view in the mirror of the loving, compassionate creature that transcends the animal thoroughly. "Omigosh, we are human!!!!"

As long as all of the nobler qualities remain undermined, we will remain a *very* destructive version of an animal; not a human, loving, thinking, emotionally balanced race of beings that can exceed all expectations.

Our humanity has been denied by erroneous conclusions and delusional machinations.   Our sentience has remained hobbled from an unexpected source.

The best of humanity follow the rules because that is the best compromise in a compromising situation.

Kudos, but there's a better way.

All of the foul behaviour that has marked humanity's existence, so far, is not necessary.

One particular situation became evident, along with our sentient state.   It causes our sentience to remain unglued until it is recognized and repaired.   We could not cope with it, so we swept it under the rug.   We used our creativity and imagination to create delusions and distractions in order to avoid ever pondering the subject that our curiosity made evident, but with which our newly minted intellect could not cope. Derailments, like "we are only human", are the result that constantly jeopardizes and undermines our sentient awareness.

Emergence

There is a single crucial feature of the human state that remains absent. Its presence will fulfill our human nature. It is uniquely human. No animal could ever replicate it. It has nothing to do with how smart we are. Its absence causes our emotional upheaval. Even though it is the simplest of realizations, we have avoided confronting it at all costs.

Humanity, alone, can look into the eyes of their lover during coitus. Funny thing. We usually turn out the lights. There is something absent that haunts that potential loving engagement.

Worse than that, the absence *and our sentient awareness of its absence* have driven us mad. As hard as we try to deny the insight, our awareness cannot be denied. We have done nothing but avoid the issue and create endless alternatives instead. For millennia we have tried to convince ourselves it is not a big deal.

That ability to perceive reality with a heightened sense and comprehension was a new add-on for the human model of animals. In one crucial instance, we used our creativity and imagination to manipulate the interpretation of reality rather than confirm and address it. It became a habit. That has caused us to misinterpret our existence in fundamental ways.

Our sentience seeks clarity in all things. Due to a single instance, for more than three thousand years, we have distorted what we sense rather than seeking clarity. That has totally disoriented our sentient loving state.

One of the attributes that we carried along from the animal was sex. Sex was something done because the *male* animal had an urgent need for sexual release and the *female* animal tolerated it due to the biological urge to procreate. That is all there is to it for an animal.

Something must drive the animal to renew itself or become extinct. Sex was the ticket. Coitus, the vehicle. It had been ongoing for a billion years when our sentience arrived to question the situation.

Sexual gratification is hit or miss for an animal. For the female, it is mostly a miss. The female's gratification is not important for an animal. They are too dimwitted to be permitted to perceive anything more.

The necessity is that the animal procreate and nothing more. Nature made sure it worked for its ultimate purpose of making babies, even for a dimwitted animal. Whether the female achieves pleasure does not even come into play for an animal.

Animals are too simple-minded to comprehend that there can be something more. That is far from true for humans. We have just avoided admitting it.

Behind so much of the human sexual landscape of contention is the desire to achieve mutual pleasure. Coitus never seemed willing to cooperate. We have never even really taken the prospect seriously. We began to seek alternatives, instead.

As humanity's awareness continues to become more conscious of the scheme of things, it becomes more evident that coitus is a quandary. It's fine for making babies but the woman's pleasure remains missing.

A woman can achieve orgasm during coitus. This is a thought that would never cross a simple animal's mind. It crosses a man's mind constantly. Its failure drives him to distraction. He feels helpless when he doesn't succeed, which is the most common result.

This unspoken awareness has been present for a very long time. We have fought that awareness as if it were some shame on humanity. The shame is that we have avoided admitting that something is missing from coitus. Only once it is admitted and faced, can it be addressed. In the meantime, we remain convinced we are no better than an animal.

Our creative faculties were used to deny the situation, instead of facing the problem in order to overcome it. We put it on the shelf for three thousand years. In the meantime, the deed was done in the dark and forgotten as soon as possible. As an example, men may regale you with their sexual exploits. It is seldom, if ever, that they will regale you with their ability to love a woman. The animal remains.

The closest we have come to addressing it is the studies that show that most men can only last a minute or three. This has been used as 'proof' that there is nothing to be done about it. Sorry, women, you're out of luck. "We are only human."

Poor men have felt helpless and hopeless. Oh so achingly slowly, they have accepted alternative ways in which to succeed. They *seem* to have tried everything but coitus just wouldn't cooperate!

Spoiler alert: Coitus can be made to cooperate really, really, really well. Men have not tried everything, after all.

We are not limited to an animal's version of coitus, we just never realized it. Men made a grave mistake equating coitus with an Olympic event. It takes a bit more than flexing one's muscles. It takes some human consideration and thought. In fact, muscle flexing is part of the problem.

Humanity has desperately avoided inspecting the coital situation with any vigour. It broke men's minds to realize that the most natural event was not as it seemed and there didn't seem to be a damned thing they could do about it except hold on for dear life and hope for the best. What a blunder. It is a blunder that has rolled down through the ages. We have been conditioned to accept it as is.

Much of the dreams of prepubescent youth are based on the expected glorious fulfillment of coitus. What a surprise and a crushing defeat when we find it is not so. Our dreams turn to ashes. We look for alternatives. None can fulfill a human like loving coitus and reveal our real human nature in full measure.

Its lack has derailed humanity since the beginning. Our sentience was crushed. We ran off in every direction in our attempts to avoid the consideration.

What would ignite if coitus, the original, natural unassisted method of sexual gratification were easily fulfilled?

Whether you are the cause of the failure, or the one experiencing the failure, that incredibly special experience is turned to ashes when both do not achieve climax regularly. The man and the woman's life, feelings of self, are damaged, disoriented. All because, long ago, our incompetent ancestors couldn't keep it up.

All of those sayings, like "we're only human" or "Life sucks and, then you die" begin to make sense. It is the wailing of an animal that is so much more than just an animal and, yet, has not attained that which provides for sentient clarity and fulfillment. We have lied to ourselves and our sentience damn well knows it.

If we could not achieve loving coitus, all of the alternatives taken in order to achieve the fulfilling satisfaction of two participants would make sense. But, we should first take a very close look at why men have failed to make coitus a fulfilling engagement. So far, all of the research and studies regarding coitus have not really made the attempt. They have been blocked by the same inertia that has forced us to look away from the challenge. "Most men last a couple of minutes, therefore, they always will." Once again, an animal's answer.

Loving coitus completes the picture of what is different about humans. The dream of loving coitus, a natural, loving sexual experience between man and woman fulfills the human landscape like nothing else. In the absence of loving coitus human life is compromised.

We sense the potential of love, honour, integrity and the whole host of finer qualities in our youth. The failure convinces us, more and more as we age, that it is no more than a pipe dream. It is no wonder. "We are only human."

We have always been awaiting resolution. In its absence, we lash out. That was *not* the way the script was written for a sentient race.

The only thing that is at all astounding is that it has taken us so very long to even articulate what is going on. That makes it crystal clear that we did not want to ever consider the subject. That is nothing short of insane.

We cannot become fully human until we admit what we already know and address the issue. The denial, the refusal to even consider that there really is something more to unassisted coitus and that humanity can do something about it, has caused our human nature to become more and more disoriented. We constantly regress to the animal. The biggest problem has always been the refusal to acknowledge the situation, not the failure itself.

Every one or two days during a great portion of a lifetime, the failure stares most of us in the face. It drives us mad.

There are very few men, if any, that can assure themselves that they can provide a woman full sexual pleasure during coitus without assistance. It has been ringing in men's ears for thousands of years. Humanity has tried to hide from the debacle but it still remains. It won't abate on its own and it continues to wreak untold havoc in the meantime.

The issue was buried so deeply so long ago that, nowadays, we never even consider that there should be something better. We seldom admit there is a problem. We accept the failure and the spirit of the sentient being withers and becomes further and further disoriented.

Now, tell me what you think will happen when we can actually celebrate the loving event rather than dread its unloving failure, over and over, again, throughout a lifetime?

For three thousand years we have had the failure drummed into us: just don't think about it. "We're only human. What problem?"

The source of the emotional upheaval in men is evident. Rather than loving a woman, a man spends most of his time covering up his failure, turning out the lights and going to sleep as quickly as possible to forget the whole thing.

Men can love just as well as women. It's born into men just as it is in women. It's just shows up dead on arrival the first time they try to love a woman. They become more and more dead inside over a lifetime. The denial is killing humanity.

Who can love someone when the most loving act of existence is reduced to a fumbling animal's rutting? As long as we can't express that love physically, we remain lost. It refutes our sentient state of conscious awareness and undermines our human nature.

It has always been like a huge abyss separating us from our humanity. Unintentionally, our sentience was derailed.

What has always stumped us, since we first became aware that man and woman can *both* achieve orgasm is how to make it the reliable outcome of unassisted coitus. The human race will never really be satisfied until that is true. We have avoided addressing the situation openly because we are certain that there is no hope of redressing the situation.

It is *not knowledge* that has been our doom. It has been lack of comprehension and purposeful subterfuge that has been the problem.

Can you even see men's dilemma? They achieve the most incredible experience of existence and see it fail for the woman with whom they share the experience. It is devastating.

It is a devastating, crushing burden. Men have always expected themselves to just face up to the situation, nose to the grindstone and all. Bitter dregs, indeed.

Loving coitus frees humanity to become human. It is the liberation, the freedom, we have always sought.

One single way in which sex can become something uniquely human and we have buried it in denial. We can look into the eyes of our lover during coitus and, yet usually, we turn out the lights.

Nature has set us up since day one to be a loving, fulfilled race of sentient beings. We set ourselves up for failure.

Nature provided the means for an intelligent, sentient recovery from the witless act of the animal. Instead, we avoid the issue and remain an animal demented by its heightened awareness.

The disparity in the physical expression of love has undermined the equality and equity of genders.

From the get-go, women were shortchanged and men knew they were responsible. What do you think that does to a sentient state of equality and equity? The stunted sentient state of humanity is the reason for armed camps between the two genders.

Men have suppressed women because they really did not want to hear about their failure. They have scrambled for ages in every way possible to avoid open realization of their failure. Suppressing women was just part of the program.

While that may enrage some women, it shouldn't. It is the comedy of errors of our past. Much more important is to correct the situation. If we couldn't, then we wouldn't deserve to be considered sentient. All of the upheaval would continue.

Men know they have failed but rather than admit it and face up to the situation, they put on airs of confidence. The surliness, the mistreatment of women, the emotional vacuum (or upheaval), the toxic masculinity, the mad desire for success at anything else as as mad substitute are all due to the failure at the most important success story, loving coitus, that men *know* is their responsibility.

We are constantly dragged back to the animal perspective because we have not learned to love in the most essential way. Failed coitus is the precursor to all of our troubles.

It is a door nailed shut that needs to be blown to bits.

The desire for *mutual* pleasure while gazing into the eyes of one's lover during the most natural expression of love can never leave a self-aware race. It drives the species irreversibly crazy as long as it is unattained.

Sharing, equality, love and all of the finer qualities begin with sharing the ultimate, most transcendent experience of human, sexual fulfillment and, thereby, maintaining one's self-respect.

Why do you think the topic of sex and coitus are so taboo? Why in the world would we not celebrate the most extraordinary experience in life, openly and with enthusiasm? The only reason is because we know damn well we have not achieved the human experience. We remain an animal.

What do you think happens when all that is shared is the failure of the experience of coitus? In case you are seriously trying to consider it, it's easier than you think. Just look around. The extremes of wackiness it causes are becoming evident, once again, across the world stage.

Generation after generation reaches puberty with such high expectations and dreams regarding coitus only to have them disappointed, crushed. Each generation learns to turn out the lights, go to sleep as quickly as possible, and forget about it by morning.

In the absence of mutually satisfying coitus, we stumble along like a blind animal. We turn out the lights, in so many ways, because we have not faced the situation.

All because the male animal couldn't keep it up and earliest humans hadn't a clue about how to change that, other than denying the whole situation vociferously, in any imaginative and creative way possible.

Early man got stuck on failure of the Olympian event and only used his mind to bury and deny the failure as deeply as possible. That is another huge part of why men continued to fail. We attacked the problem as an animal would. Otherwise, it would not have taken three thousand years to figure out just how easily a man can last indefinitely.

Men *take* pleasure and women *give* pleasure during coitus. That defines the human state that remains an animal's witless existence. Women give and men take. That works fine for a witless animal. It does not work for a highly aware, highly sensitized, sentient race.

Our human nature has been so obliterated that most will not even openly admit there is a problem or that the potential of the human race remains broken. After all, "we're only human", they whine.

A gross misconception provided by that defeat is that our finer qualities need to be learned. Just like Pavlov's Dog, we believe we need to be trained to be human. Instead of our finer qualities being nurtured from birth, they are crushed out of men as they reach puberty and fail at the most extraordinary act of being human.

Human nature is far and away different from the current human condition of fiction and delusion. Our assessment that humanity needs to *learn* to be human is wrong. Sure, we need to acquire knowledge and understanding but our essential human nature remains missing. It *can't* be learned. It is a gift that Nature provided and humanity has constantly undermined because of the issue being described.

Loving coitus, the most intimate form of love (arguably the most important feature of sentient existence) can fuse a man and woman into something more. It will reveal our human nature.

The only real challenge is to unlock the key to make it a loving event. I have gone a long way towards uncovering that which has always remained hidden due to our stupefaction. A sentient race *can* make coitus a *naturally* (e.g. no pills, etc) loving event.

Intimate relationships have become like a revolving door of sexual partners rather than a lifelong bond in which the relationship relies on cherishing one another and grows throughout a lifetime.

Do you think loving coitus might make a difference? What do you really think is the real source of all of those petty arguments and snipes that couples endure from each other? Some may make a good show of loving each other but I wonder if there are any that achieve the true bliss of fusion?

We have become inured to the ongoing failure, the high divorce rate, and the rest of the absurdity of an existence that does not match our expectations or our human nature.

Humanity continues to chase the dream while the individual is trapped in failure. After enough failed attempts at that most intimate relationship, everyone settles for less.

Maybe, initially, for the human, it was just a vague, uncomfortable sense that something wasn't working as well as it should. But, how could something be wrong regarding coitus? Animals had done it for a billion years before humanity arrived on the scene. That was way too much for our earliest ancestors to comprehend, so they prevaricated and disavowed that there was any problem. Sex was sex. They just cursed it.

A woman's sexual satisfaction remains hit or miss during coitus. Mostly miss. It became something that one did not mention or consider, since it became erroneously clear that there was no good solution and no point in embarrassing the poor male.

At that point, our attempts at a sentient, respectable human way of life went completely off the rails.

Sexual satisfaction for the woman during coitus is predicated on the duration of the sexual experience. Without a man lasting around ten minutes or more at coitus, the woman's orgasm, generally, will not happen. That the man can last as long as necessary was just incomprehensible.

Leading into Details

All of the books that I have written over the last twelve years are about the fact that men never learned to transform the act that creates life into an act that also creates love. That has resulted in damage to the human race's development as a sentient race.

The male *gender, not a few individuals*, needs to learn that men can learn to love - easily. It needs to become firmly implanted into the brain of the human species. In other words, the human consciousness must become certain of the fact.

Have you had "that talk" with your father yet? How did it go? Did he fumble around and never say anything of import? Was he utterly relieved when you told him, it's okay, dad, I know all about it. Which you didn't.

Don't hold it against him. I'm not sure any man has really known how to love a woman physically before. They've usually known what the animal passed on to us. Rut. Stick it in and get it over with. Maybe think about baseball. Some may have actually stumbled onto a way to last long enough. That is not the same as the human potential to completely understand the situation and overcome the limitations of the animal with full awareness.

I am all about simplifying what I am trying to say. Even so, it is just such a complicated picture - in that we have been taught wrong about essentially everything for three thousand years - It has taken me writing eleven books to understand thoroughly and explain. I am on my twelfth and final book.

We have made a mess of our sentient aware existence.

The easiest part to understand is how to love a woman physically in the most elegant manner possible. The loving and human version of coitus. It is the implications, obfuscations, and refutations regarding this uniquely human, sentient experience that has made the rest so complicated.

The saying goes that men want sex and women want love. That portrays the dilemma poorly. Men *settle* for sex, in utter frustration, because they have not been able to fulfill the act of love the way they have always desperately desired to do and Nature always intended to make a unique sentient experience.

This is about how a man learns he can last long enough to make coitus a loving, human, sentient, fulfilling event. This is all about how a man learns that he is not held hostage by an animal's instincts, low grade thinking, and a dim-witted brutish approach to life. This is all about how a man learns that he is not just an animal.

A man does not differentiate himself from an animal until he realizes that he can love. That is unique to humans and loving coitus bridges the gap. He doesn't learn to love fully until he can express that love in its physical form in the way Nature provided. Anything less is a disappointment. It is the only purely human sexual act. Eye to eye, celebrating life and love.

Early male humans equated themselves with animals and conducted themselves as such. They took a craven approach to life that has remained, in great part, to this day.

Today's male humans remain mystified by their failure. They have accepted it as such because that is how it has always been. The leap to see beyond the paradigms that broke our humanity are formidable. The act itself is simple.

I've learned a lot since the initial insight of "Don't twerk or jerk until the lady sings" and made it all available in most of the books starting with *Millennium* (my favorite).

Details

Number one. A man is not on a countdown clock in any way when it comes to coitus. Only animals are. That mistaken belief has stopped the male gender in its tracks for so long. The belief is that, once you are aroused and penetrate, the ejaculation process is off and running. That is true for an animal. It is not true of a human.

The huge mistake compounded by that belief is that the best you can do is hold on for dear life as you helplessly watch the tidal wave of ejaculate makes its way downstream. Let me be crystal clear. Any way in which you attempt hold back the tide, once begun, is bad. It can cause damage.

So, no, you are not on a clock and it is not a good idea to try to hold back the process of ejaculation, once begun in earnest. If you catch it early enough, you can stop all activity long enough for things to settle down. Some refer to this as edging. It works. Keep it in your toolbox for making love, but don't expect to use it except as you are learning to master your body. Forget master of the universe. Master of your body is far more fulfilling.

What really works is to understand why the process of ejaculation gets started and what can be done about it so that you become a master of your own body. It's not magic. You are only held back by the witless instincts of an animal that have never been investigated fully in any way before.

There is only one thing that gets the ejaculation process started. Squeezing the sex glands in the bottom of your crotch, your pelvic region. *That* begins the process. Nothing else.

What happens is that the glands gets squeezed by two events, the muscles and/or the musculoskeletal structure in the pelvic region. The squeezing can be avoided. They are squeezed due to following the instincts of an animal without even realizing it.

There is one condition in which there is no stopping it. It will not be stopped if the glands are overfull. It is already being squeezed by being overfull. The solution is obvious.

Otherwise, two primary instincts cause the beginning of the end. One is simple to understand and control. That is the effect of the musculoskeletal structure of the pelvic region. The other is overcome by mastering the muscles in the pelvic region of your body. It's not difficult to do. It was just difficult to unravel.

There is a desire to immediately plunge as deeply into that heavenly place, as you can. Save it for the grand finale. Doing so forces the musculoskeletal structure around the pelvic region into a position to squeeze the glands. It best to remain as shallow as possible until you learn what you are doing.

All of the woman's erotic nerve endings are within two inches or less of the opening, anyways. The erogenous zone with the most erotic nerve endings is the clitoral nub which is located about half an inch *outside* of the vagina. If you do no stimulate this clitoris button, it is unlikely you will be stimulating the woman enough to achieve own orgasm. More details later.

The one that is more difficult to comprehend is how the muscles in your crotch operate. The more I study it, the more convinced I become that within two or three generations, without all of the impediments that are currently thrown into our faces, like the bad habits acquired, the missing knowledge, and the expectation of failure, combined with a growing confidence by the male gender, will make it as easy as learning to ride a bike. It is a different effort.

You have to teach yourself to master those muscles and not use them. It is not difficult. It is just that we never tried because we always veer completely away from any thoughts on the matter due to the paralyzing fear of admitting failure.

The muscles in your crotch, your pelvic muscles, will squeeze the sex glands if flexed. *They don't need to.* Those muscles only contract because we never thought about it. We react like an animal without thought. Animals contract those muscles because they have the wit of, well, an animal.

The pelvic muscles have nothing to do with movement and, yet, during the movement of coital engagement, they contract and relax because we just don't think about it. We've never trained the muscles.

It's easy to prove. Try moving any part of your body by using only your pelvic muscles. You can't do it. They are not attached in that way. They are not muscles for moving. They are attached in a way that controls the output of bodily fluids. In the case of ejaculate, flexing the pelvic muscles, during tumescence, will start the process of ejaculation by squeezing the sex glands.

During coitus, you have to learn to move your body *without* contracting the pelvic muscles. It's not really a big deal, once you become familiar with the idea. It's not like trying to master the heart muscles (which also can be done to some extent; i guess some may even be able to stop the heart completely. it's just that you never hear about it because they are dead).

The pelvic muscles are not needed at all during coitus. It is just a matter of learning to move the body without allowing those muscles to flex. It may be helpful to use them when the woman says it's time to end it, but I am not even certain that it will ever be necessary. A deep dive is the best, most satisfying, and certain trigger. It is a nearly unavoidable trigger, which is why it is so commonly used before it is necessary.

This is why I came up with the phrase early on, "don't twerk or jerk until the lady sings." It's trite but it gets many points across. It points out, for instance, a most critical necessary point of control for the pelvic muscles. When changing directions, especially on the backstroke when you are withdrawing, it is *very* easy to let those muscles contract until well-trained. There is a tendency to jerk.

There is a third effect that needs to be considered but it is part of mastering the muscles, and not nearly as difficult. That is the erotic sensation. This is how the head of the penis gets involved. The erotic sensations that can blow your mind can also trigger a spasming contraction of those muscles.

In essence, it is no different than the tickling sensation in other parts of your body. You can master the spasming by exercising those muscles, making them more supple and responsive. Don't freak out. It should take more more than a couple of minutes a day to train them, maybe less for someone that matures into his sexuality already knowing what to do.

Those muscles, essentially, have never been consciously controlled or trained and made supple. In fact, you can control the muscles reaction to tickling in any part of the body, if necessary. (i had a cruel older sister. i know). You can control any tickling sensation. If anything, it makes the enhanced experience more mind-blowing.

Once you master those muscles, some intriguing possibilities begin to present themselves. As I mentioned, the erotic zones of the woman are all very close to the opening. The most important, the clitoral nub, is about a half-inch outside and above the vagina. This nub, or button, has far more erotic nerve endings than even the head of your penis.

Without stimulating this, it is unlikely you will bring the woman to the point of orgasm. One has to pay attention in order to stroke the nub because of its position. One has to position oneself in such a way to stroke outside and above the vagina with the shaft of the penis. Make sure you know if you are stimulating acceptably.

The rest of the clitoris erogenous zone, the clitoral wishbone, surrounds the vagina just inside the walls of the opening. This is the other most important erotic zone for the woman.

While it is not a challenge to stroke with the shaft, bringing the head of the penis into contact with the clitoral wishbone is another level of stimulation for the woman. Do not even attempt it until you have mastered the basics discussed above.

Bang! You are now human. You should be able to learn to last as long as *she* desires. You can finally feel successful at the most transcendent act of human life.

I wish I could be around for the next hundred years or so, as all of this flourishes. I just know there are mountains more learning that will occur once men's terrible inhibitions, frustrations, and emasculations are shredded as loving coitus truly and finally becomes celebrated as it always should have been and is transformed into a loving art form.

It is the most important art form of love that will replace the grubbing ways in which sex is treated today.

I've had many women mention how it is all about the missing affection in men that is the problem. That is what drives women crazy and away. What women have never realized is that missing affection stems from the same problem.

How can a man not become inhibited in his expression of affection and love as he fails at the most essential act of making love? How can he maintain an affectionate demeanor when failing to express it in the most meaningful way in bed?

The man may feel utterly disappointed in the situation, as well as himself, feeling like he has already betrayed the woman he desires to show his love. Many a man will close up, once his failure to express his love in the most meaningful physical manner begins to sink in. It sinks in so insidiously many never even become aware of it. It can become a haunting feel that won't go away but, also, won't surface.

Yes, some overcome the shock. Some find other ways. You cannot tell me they are not disappointed all the same.

Men take, women give and it all starts in bed. It doesn't need to remain that way.

I will say, once again, kudos to guys that find some other way to satisfy their partner, kudos to those that have taken a completely different route to find love. I'm sure your affection is far more than those that never learned to love in whatever way is possible and works best for the couple. But, still, until loving coitus is a reality that mankind accepts and proliferates, it is a humbled existence at which any primate could succeed. Only with loving coitus do we separate ourselves decisively from the animals.

I mention exercises. It is in some detail below. There are also plenty of Kegel exercises available on the web. Just keep in mind that there are two parts to the exercise. The second will not be mentioned in any reference to Kegel exercises. The first is to exercise those muscles to make them supple and responsive. The *second* is to *not* exercise those muscles while exercising the muscles that are *meant* for movement in your thighs, torso, etc. in order to become familiar with the separation of efforts. I like my exercises better because they only take a couple of minutes.

Regarding masturbation (I explain more below). Do not abuse your member. That is even worse than any bad habits you can pick up from masturbation. On bad habits, do not let the habit of thinking only about your own causing your own orgasm during masturbation prevent you from thinking about the woman's during the actual event of coitus.

Your main goal *has* to be the woman's orgasm during coitus. You orgasm is assured, hers is not. Habits are hard to break.

I have left as much of my original details below because I am concerned that this is a difficult enough subject as it is. Reiteration in different words may help. I have not edited much.

Original Details

Men have always accepted that starting the process of ejaculation was impossible to avoid. Because of this misconception, it became a matter of attempting to *stop the end result*. **Big mistake.** That is far too late. It became something similar to an olympic event in most men's minds. More strength is not the answer. More control is.

The big picture is that the sex glands in the crotch, when squeezed, begin ejaculation. Nothing else. That's it.

Two instincts trigger the sex glands by squeezing them. It has been 'a mystery' before now. So much for mystery.

Men learned only to hold on for dear life *after* the process of ejaculation has already begun. That assures the two or three minute limit that is de rigueur in sex studies. A study of the anatomy and the characteristics of the act of coitus is much more enlightening. There is no limit.

The unfortunate results of uncontrolled ejaculation ends the act of coitus before it can ever become a loving, thereby, human event that creates the loving environment that is necessary to fulfill our humanity. Uncontrolled ejaculation is a disaster. It is prehuman. It is not necessary and highly destructive to relationships and the human race.

By studying the anatomy in the context of erection, ejaculation and some of the oddities of results of masturbation, it becomes clear. Squeezing the sex glands in the pubic area (i.e. the crotch, the pelvic region) begins the process of ejaculate discharge.

There are two instinctual reactions that cause the witless squeezing of the sex glands in the crotch. They is nothing more than the instincts of the animals that came before us. That knowledge has been shunted aside due to the overwhelming feelings of shame that were first encountered by the first fully awakened sentient intellect more than three millennia ago. Those instincts, when the shame is shunted aside and the intellect finally assesses the real situation, are easy to overcome because we are human, thinking creatures.

One of those instincts is as simple to overcome as it is to understand. Men don't twerk until the lady sings. Thrusting the pubic bone (crotch) forward to the furthest extent squeezes the glands decisively (i.e. twerking). The animal's *instinct* is to immediately plunge as deeply as possible. It just feels good.

In the case of twerking (undisciplined full forward thrust), the musculoskeletal structure forces the pubic bone into a position that squeezes the sex glands. It will invariably cause the beginnings of orgasm, and ejaculation in the man's case.

The second instinct is more subtle. The pelvic muscles *are not required for movement.* They have everything to do with squeezing the sex glands and controlling other bodily output functions. The pelvic muscles do not *need* to flex, unless desired, during the movements of sexual activity. When flexed, they squeeze the sex glands.

The other muscles in the thighs, buttocks, back, and torso, etc are the only necessary muscles for movement. The crotch muscles only flex due to the witless instincts of the animal. They don't do anything regarding movement. They are not used for movement, they just witlessly follow along.

It is just a matter of realizing this and avoiding using the pelvic muscles for the movements involved in loving coitus. This is what I term 'jerking'. It just takes practice.

The two endpoints of the stroke are the most likely to cause those muscles to flex inadvertently, which is where the term jerking originated.

It's not so much leaving them lax as *not flexing them.* Flexing and relaxing those muscles acts like a pump on the glands. The 'tickling' effect on the head of the penis cause the same results through spasming. Mastery of these muscles is key.

The muscle response (jerking) or deep plunge (twerking) squeezes the glands containing the fluids that begins the cascade to orgasm. Save the deep plunge for the finale, when *she* is ready. It will *always* cause ejaculation and orgasm on call within a very short period of time. You can learn how long, also, with practice. It can all be controlled.

Holding on for dear life is *exactly* what a man does *not* want to do as it amounts to *flexing the pelvic muscles*!

One additional critical point. If the glands are <u>already overfull</u>, squeezing the glands is unavoidable. The solution is obvious.

Only about two inches is required to stroke the woman's every erotic nerve-ending inside and out, while allowing the head of the penis to remain fully inside the vagina. The shaft itself strokes the most sensitive arousal point (i.e. clitoral nub) that is just *outside* and *above* the opening (by ~ one-half inch or less).

The other major erogenous zone for a woman is the clitoral wishbone, much less than two inches inside.

Stroking the clitoral wishbone, just inside the vaginal opening, with the flaring portion of the head will also help stimulate the woman. That may be best saved for after you have learned the basics. The woman's twerking should assist her orgasm in the same way as a man. The two should discuss what works best.

Think on this. Now, once you both begin to achieve orgasm, you can leave the lights on and look into each other's loving eyes as you each achieve the transcendent state of orgasm.

Just be careful and go very slow until you understand 1) how deep is safe (it should be far more than two inches as you progress in your learnings) and 2) how to avoid contracting (or, worse, spasming) the muscles in the crotch.

An additional technique, if necessary, is to stop all activity at the first sign that you are becoming overstimulated until the sense of overstimulation is gone. It should not be necessary with exercise and practice but may be useful while still learning.

It is a learning process. We are human. That is what we do. That is what we are *supposed* to do. In the case of coitus, we have avoided the learning process, thus remaining a dumbfounded animal.

These points are straightforward and will become as natural as the instincts and animal responses that they replace within a generation or two of the time that humanity begins to succeed at love in its most essential physical form. Little real learning should be necessary within a generation or two. It will be absorbed from the confidence of one's elders (which is completely missing today) and, maybe, a few minor insights that will be commonly known, like, "don't twerk, don't jerk, and exercise. Become familiar with the muscles in the crotch and *don't flex them*. Make them supple."

The exercises are just as crucial for loving coitus in youth as it is for later in life. There are other benefits as you age, like not wearing diapers. The immediate advantages, even in youth, include making it easier to master the muscles and any untoward spasming of the muscles. It will take some slight effort and discipline, as well as exercise (two minutes!), to avoid flexing and spasming. Avoiding the deep plunge is just a matter of paying attention. Now, you will be able to open your eyes to the one you adore while actually loving her in the best way.

I spend around *two* minutes (only two!) exercising those muscles daily, and, also, practicing *not* flexing them by only exercising the muscles that *are* necessary for movement.

On your back with knees flexed, swing your knees towards each other and away. Flex the pelvic muscles as you swing the knees towards each other. Relax the muscles as you swing the knees apart. Thirty times, approximately thirty seconds. This will make the muscles supple and help you become familiar with muscles. Then, flex another thirty times while swinging the knees in and out. In this case, leave the crotch muscles relaxed while working only the leg, butt, and hip muscles to get the pelvic muscles familiar with avoiding flexing while the the muscles meant for movement are working. This could also be practiced during walking, sitting, or any form of exercise, though I found it best to be able to concentrate. I've also experimented with variations a bit. One that is intriguing is flexing the pelvic muscles on one count, then leaving them relaxed on the next.

Then, I hold them for a count of five, relax, another five count, relax. Six of these total.

I would also suggest alternating between this exercise and doing them with the legs stretched out fully. Just swinging your toes suffice, in this case.

Another good, errr, non-exercise is standing knee bends *without* flexing the pelvic muscles. What is termed 'sexercise' would be a perfect time to practice this. Tai chi or squats work just as well.

In essence, you are trying to do two things. Condition the pelvic muscles *and* become familiar with *not* using them when unnecessary and detrimental to the act of loving coitus.

I really doubt this will be the last written on exercises to make it easier to avoid unwanted orgasms. I have already rewritten this a dozen times as I learned more and more. I expect there is more yet that others will discover once we remove the blinders.

Another caution. Self-stimulation (or dress rehearsals, or masturbation, if you prefer) needs to be done carefully for the man. If you abuse your member, it will come back to haunt you. *Do not inadvertently do so!* It will make it almost impossible to avoid the beginnings of ejaculation. There is no reason to abuse your member, *if you realize what triggers an orgasm.*

It can be difficult to achieve orgasm when, errr, taking the matter in hand, *because* the normal motions of coitus are *not* the norm during self-stimulation. Also, the tickle response is absent.

A person cannot tickle themselves.

Also, the urge to rush through can become a habit that follows through when attempting to last as long as *she* desires. Do not allow that habit to develop. It is really hard to break. If one uses something other than one's hand, it may be possible to engage the tickle response to some extent and begin to overcome it.

Abuse, which can happen in attempts to cause the tickle response, or rush to completion, will make the spasm response *extremely* difficult to overcome. *Do not abuse your member.*

Humanity should learn to approach masturbation unabashedly. It is far better than letting the lack of release get under one's skin. I'm not expecting that to change in a hurry. Once we lose our sense of shame regarding sex, maybe we will have a chance.

Also, don't let your child (either sex, really) be mutilated by circumcision. In the U.S., it is considered a Christian tradition. IT IS NOT A CHRISTIAN TRADITION!!!! The health aspect is also a crock. It is sadistic. It leaves scars.

There is no rational reason for the mutilation of circumcision (either gender), though there are many irrational, insane reasons.

A circumcised person can still achieve controlled ejaculation but it may be more of a challenge (I was circumcised).

More importantly, the biggest thing for me is that I am certain it leaves a psychic shock when they slice it away, no matter the anesthetics or sharpness of the scalpel. There's just no need for it. It is sick and sadistic. It is an animal reveling in causing pain.

I would say that, no matter where you are in the world, it would be worth checking before you have a baby. In many places (the U.S. south), they will slice without asking.

Just remember, you are human. Of course you can control the muscles and your own discharge. Keep in mind that overfull glands means they *will* be squeezed and it will be over in a hurry. How you handle that is up to you.

Do not become discouraged if it takes a little while to adjust and make things work. At this point, it is all new. The older you are, the more time should be expected in order to adjust as there are more bad habits necessary to overcome.

You can now proceed to engage in loving coitus, mutual orgasm, enthusiastically in a human manner while gazing into your lover's eyes with the lights on. Love can finally mature into its sentient form. We can become human. Rather than a porn-watching subhuman race. I apologize for concentrating on the men's issues but men have the most to learn, by far.

There is another point that I have not highlighted before. The closest I came was mentioning that, after men gain their confidence, their self-respect, the rest will come easily.

While that is true, it is not enough, at this point. During the transition into that state, there are a few things that a man will need to consider. After we are human, it will be as obvious as the Earth beneath your feet.

Not only does a woman's orgasm take some time but, at least at this point, so does arousal for many women. I think it is very possible that this, also, will change, once women become convinced that they, also, can expect to achieve orgasm during coitus on a consistent basis. Their enthusiasm may often even match that of the man.

The point is that, if a man does not take his time achieving the woman's high arousal, before beginning coitus, she may never achieve orgasm. I would love to see a book by a woman on these matters. The orientation for a man needs to change radically. It is not all about him. It is all about loving and giving, not just pleasing oneself.

For women, just make sure you are doing the opposite of what I've recommended for men and you should orgasm easily. Flex and twerk like crazy or as much as he can bear, which should improve over time. Relish the erotic feelings that cause the spasms to engage. Again, I would dearly love to see a woman write a book on the woman's sexual situation and insights.

I am becoming more and more convinced that, as we open up and become more comfortable with the change and the insights, we will learn a lot more.

All of this will become natural once we remove the blinders. We will no longer be in hiding, and we can look for further ways in which to improve the loving. I don't mean just the physical aspects, either. This book will become unnecessary soon.

As an example of the other aspects to explore further, I'll mention romance and, of course, foreplay. Those are other natural aspects of being human that have been inhibited by men's inability to love physically, his shame.

Once our natural desire to love is established and reinforced by men gaining confidence that they can love, the rest of our loving nature will flourish. This goes well beyond the intimate relationship, as well. Humanity can become a balanced, emotionally stable, rational loving race of sentient beings without the over-heightened paranoia and despair.

A few further notes as I progress even further. First of all, after six books I am annoyed to find that the excellent term that I had created, indefinitely delayed ejaculation, 1) is not unique, and 2) has been already adopted to cover the case of the poor man that can't ever ejaculate or, goodness forbid (yeah, still despise using the term 'god' in any form), might last long enough to pleasure his woman with orgasm.

Secondly, there is a lot better term: controlled ejaculation.

I haven't even touched on any of the subjects besides men lasting long enough that are crucial to making love. The rest of it will come easily, once men are certain that they don't need to fail at the most essential task: lasting long enough. In the meantime, though, as we seek our way, it is at least worth mentioning a few key points.

The rest is easy, if you consider it at all, but still worth noting. The emotional loving, the affectionate responses and attitudes; the romance, the foreplay, the loving attitude, the gentle, equitable treatment of women, the rainbow loving of women that has been lacking, all falls right out of what I have been explaining. Men must just put their shame behind them.

Also, remember, it is the woman that gets pregnant, not you. So, if coitus is off the table, deal with it. If you care for her enough, you'll stick around. Find some other way in which to achieve mutual orgasm.

I have to highlight, though, that there are other ways to *assure* (a condom is not assurance; the woman being forced to futz with her hormones by taking a pill is not, either, besides, futzing with her physiology and mental state) impregnation never takes place while engaging in coitus.

Admissions and extensions

Everything above in this chapter has been proved to my own satisfaction. It was more difficult than most any man should encounter from this point forward. That is the point in explaining all of this. The effort is not difficult. Just overcoming the brainwashing and avoidance of the issue was difficult.

In a number of ways, it was more difficult for me. I had no template. I was encumbered by all of the lies, misdirections, and utter suppression of the subject that have burdened mankind for millennia. I was also circumcised. I also had damage to the head of my penis prepubescence and, worst of all, I had abused my member.

I have now provided a basic template to move forward and avoid all of the pitfalls that I encountered over a lifetime *before* I realized it was all a sham almost too late to prove the case to myself.

I realize this does not prove the case for all men. That will take some time and effort by others to show that it is not an isolated case and expand on the basic template that I have provided. The point of the previous two paragraphs is to emphasize that I am no one special when it comes to making loving coitus.

Everything I have to add, from this point forward, regarding improving men's performance to the point that they are in full control of the body when it comes to controlling, errr, coming, and mastering their bodies has no proof, other than I have spent the last dozen years pondering it all and linking many, many obscure dots.

These insights came far too late for me to prove them out with any level of certainty. I have no proof they help but they are rational considerations, in some cases, extrapolations from previous insights *that did work*. Some, points below, are just clarifications.

I am way to friggin' old now to be able to 'test them out' with any validity. But, they make sense.

I have to start by stressing that we are only just beginning, so there will be a lot more to learn as we progress and shed the blinders.

Humanity never stops improving on anything that it (finally) takes seriously. Loving coitus will become far more than the clinical analysis that I have had to provide. It will become art. It will expand the art of loving into something more human, once the unnecessary fear and shame are put away.

None of this will be necessary at all as men begin to gain confidence in their ability to love.

It's just that hangover of deluding ourselves for three millennia that continues to concern me. So, the more thorough the explanation and understanding, the easier it will be for all men to get over the hurdle of the debacle of our past that has prevented the human race from loving fully.

On the topic of exercise, I want to stress *not* to follow any rule book. You may start with my suggestions but find what works best for you. I would be shocked in the extreme if people don't find even better ways to strengthen and train those muscles.

I lost along the way through the many books one interesting technique that can be used while learning to master one's body. Moving the whole body, rather than flexing the hips in any way, or not moving any portion of the *man's* body are two ways to avoid squeezing those glands. I'll leave it at that for your exploration. Then, the one element of spasming in response to the erotic sensation can be concentrated on.

Sometimes I think of it like this door that men have always considered locked against them. Now, as we push gently against it, we find it is wide open. Quit letting the fears of your ancient ancestors prevent you from realizing you are a human. You can love a woman the way you have always desired.

One of the most crucial points that I cannot emphasize enough is that it is about a man changing his focus and, thereby, his behaviour from that of an animal to that of a human. That is the real point of all of this. Men's humanity has been hampered.

The laser focus for every man needs to become that it is about *sharing* the love in its physical form. All of the myriad forms of love can flourish from that point forward.

This is where the discussion becomes more speculative. As I mentioned with twerking, it is the whole musculoskeletal structure that kicks in to squeeze those glands in your crotch. I think there may be another way in which the musculoskeletal structure can be persuaded to avoid putting pressure on those glands.

Men often have a tendency to point their feet at an angle with the toes away from each other. I think there is a distinct possibility that one's toes being closer together than one's heels might very well cause the musculoskeletal structure to become less prone to squeezing the sex glands. It seems like it makes more room for the glands.

More so, as I studied it further, it strengthens the muscles on the inside of the thigh if one walks with the toes pointed slightly inward.

I have another exercise that I do. It is bending at the hips with the legs and back straight. When doing the exercise with the toes closer together than the heels, I can feel those back, inner thigh muscles stretching. I am beginning to believe that these muscles also need to be strengthened in order to make it easier to avoid using the crotch muscles during coitus. Just a theory.

I would appreciate a word if things begin to start working better for you. As I have said, I am the only verified person to succeed at this, so far.

Definitively human love

The experience of loving coitus is human and involves emotions. The experience of human love cannot be taught. It is an emotional experience. It is not a matter of will or intellect. One can't will themselves to be loving. One can only will themselves to *act* loving. That is not the same and it falls by the wayside like a shot with any disturbance, unlike the real thing. The real thing is backed by self-confidence and respect.

Providing for another is central to love. So, how do you think a man feels when he can't?

The best that can be expected without shared physical loving is a disciplined approach to life. That is a sad, far cry from a loving existence. The fulfilling experience of love begins with loving emotions provided by shared sexual fulfillment.

A loving perspective is a matter of fulfillment. Browbeating people into *acting* human is not the same as *being* human.

Our emotions are unstable because we have misled ourselves, blinding our sentient awareness in so many ways.

The experience to which everyone looks forward with prepubescent high expectations only exacerbates the misery as failure is experienced.

Of course, we are emotionally unstable! The experience should complete us. Instead, the failure makes us miserable and reinforces the delusions that we are no more than a very miserable animal.

The physical act of human, sentient love, face to face, eye to eye is the absolutely most intimate engagement possible between two humans.

Eye to eye sexual engagement can only be performed by a human. More than that, only a human can learn to change its actions in order to make coitus suitable for a sentient race.

Loving coitus makes a distinction between achieving only one's own satisfaction and the satisfaction of fulfilling one's mate. Women have known the feeling of fulfilling one's mate all along. Men have learned the opposite lesson. Fulfill oneself. It's not like that is their desire. It is just how it worked out. It bent the male population in the most unfortunate and destructive manner.

Loving coitus cannot be performed by a lesser animal than humanity. Eye to eye coitus does not even exist in all but one of the lesser animals. When coitus does not complete the eye to eye engagement, we are undone.

One of the most incongruous eventualities of the ongoing fiasco is the shame and guilt that surrounds so much regarding sex. It often translates into the belief that sex itself is shameful. The latest interpretation has become "anything goes" - except loving coitus.

We have never considered that it is the failure to make coitus into a human endeavor that initiated the shame. We shrug our shoulders considering the failure a minor disturbance. It is the disturbance that rocks our existence to its core, leaving no foundation for our sentient state. I've gone into these strange distortions of the sexual landscape in detail in the previous books.

But, let's consider one point. Because the one most loving act between humans has failed miserably for thousands of years, the unacknowledged shame has encouraged perversions.

How screwed up in the head are we regarding sex? Let me count a few of the ways. Rape, pedophilia, sex trade, domestic abuse (in so many forms), porn, Marquis de Sade, to name just a few of the worst travesties we have made of sex. Perversions exist of every conceivable flavor and they are all the result of humanity remaining screwed up regarding the importance of mutual gratification. The ultimate form of which would be loving coitus. The violent perversions are only a few of the most direct ways in which it has scuttled our sentient state.

Since we couldn't get coitus right, we continued to try everything in the book to satiate the desperate biological requirement of sex without regard to its sentient fulfillment. What really scuttled our sentience, though, was our inability to face the failure of coitus to provide mutual sexual fulfillment squarely. Our sentient awareness, perforce, overrides our desire to blot it all out. As hard as we try, our sentient awareness does not allow us to look away.

Remarkably, for thousands of years, coitus has remained the act of an animal. While we struggled to make sex human, we turned a blind eye to coitus. That is extreme irony. That which can completely fulfill our humanity has been avoided like a plague.

Just consider gazing into the eyes of your lover while each of you achieves the most transcendent feeling in existence. I'm sorry but that's special and for humans only. No animal can touch it. Today, we turn out the lights.

While there is one animal that performs sex eye-to-eye, no animal attempts to please their sex partner. They are too witless to care. That is a huge difference.

Of course men care! They are sentient! In its stead, men adopt a bizarre facade of manliness that is anything but manly. Even men admitting there is a problem and finding another way to pleasure a woman would end the bizarre facade of manliness.

That mutual physical fulfillment unleashes the emotional fulfillment in full measure.

It's just not possible for a man to move past the fact that he has never really fulfilled the loving effort. How can he? Human sentience is relentless.

Like his meager attempt at manhood, his love also remains uninspired and withers away. At best, it remains a shadow of human, sentient love.

Shame and guilt have become way too common for humanity. It is reflected in so much that we endure.

Love is definitively human. Mutually satisfying coitus initiates and establishes a loving environment.

Loving, *making love*, makes us human. Love is the result. Love is about fulfillment of the other. It is hampered in both when it is not fulfilled.

In our youth, most folks have these incredibly high expectations for love, sex and the opposite sex. We convince ourselves over a lifetime that they are but a dream. The dream is often crushed even earlier by viewing the awful antics of adults.

The failure of our sentient state has become more and more evident as we become more and more fully aware.

We have convinced ourselves over the last three millennia that all the hopes of youth, rather than the adult misery and failure, are the problem. We morph from those high expectations to accommodate an animal's reality. I think a decent interpretation of the existing mantra is, "Sex is easy to find. Love, not so much."

We embrace the misery like an old friend. It is so crazy. It is all due to a misunderstanding. Crazy.

Refutations

The current concepts and considerations regarding love are all foolishness. Love should be easy to find and easy to maintain for a lifetime. The only thing impeding that is a loving physical relationship. I could go on and on explaining this but let's just look at one oddity of our current sexual situation.

The saying goes that the woman is looking for love and the man is looking for sex. Now, do you see why that is true and why it should not remain true? Do you see the nonsense behind the statement? The admission? While it is true, it should not remain true. It is true for an animal, not a human.

Loving, not just caring with occasional sex on the side, but a tremendous, transcendent experience between two people, engaged in eye to eye coitus, *will* bring them closer. How could it not? The failure repels them into the corners of their armed camps. Any form of mutual sexual gratification is like declaring a truce.

Even as miserable as the current results are, we indulge often, until the reality of the miserable situation begins to hit home. Then, it all begins to fall apart and continues to do so for the rest of a person's life.

Tell me that real, loving relationships between a man and a woman, that the great majority of humans would prefer (if it worked right), rather than the paltry excuses for remaining together in spite of the situation, wouldn't transform humanity. Loving maintained by mutually satisfying coitus, the dream of most every youth, completes our journey to sentience. It provides clarity.

We have each had our hopes for love dashed so resoundingly in our past that we resort to all kinds of excuses and explanations to justify our situation. We learn to expect and accept less from love and the physical relationship. And, of course, we inadvertently and unavoidably pass on that misery to the next generation in spectacular form until we at least admit to the problem and find some way to circumvent it.

Spectacular disasters

There's another thing I must reiterate, and expand upon, from *Sentience*. The current techniques for stopping ejaculation all rely on stopping the flow of semen at the very last moment, after the process has already begun and the flood is about to burst. A man is, essentially, attempting to hold back a tidal wave. The resultant damage is similar.

First of all, that's really stupid, once you think about it and, yet, we have followed that route to failure for millennia, even though the pitiful results have been known for just as long. Some of the more stupid techniques like putting something (like a ring) around the penis to choke off the flow, are a disaster for the normal operation of the human body.

And, of course, the practice itself emphasizes that we damn well know there is a problem with delaying ejaculation and we damn well want to last indefinitely, whether we want to admit it or not. The problem has always been addressed as an animal would. Stupidly.

The real disaster is that, if the flow doesn't go where it is supposed to, it's going seek the next weakest target. That is the bladder. Basically, one is messing with the flow controls of the body and compromising the valves *if you try to cut off the flow of ejaculate after it has begun*.

This seems to also be true of less effective methods, like just holding on ("I think I can, I think I can" method) as long as you can (one minute? two? four?) until the dam bursts.

"Desirable" coitus

There was an article regarding a survey from Penn State that I loved. It really explains a lot if one reads between the lines.

It was a survey of sex therapists regarding what was an acceptable duration for intercourse to last. The answers (*from therapists*) were 3 to 7 minutes was "acceptable"; 7 to 13 was called desirable; 1 to 2 minutes too short; 10 to 30, too long.

I put quotations marks around "acceptable" because, to me, it and the term, desirable, indicates so much regarding the direct delusions created by our inept sexual situation. Just like the term, premature ejaculation, it highlights how desperately we attempt to avoid the truth.

The woman gets well aroused at 3 to 7 minutes, but still does not usually reach climax. That is deemed "acceptable". In what world does getting slightly aroused equate with acceptable? Desirable, 7 to 13, minutes, indicates full satisfaction.

3 to 7 minutes, in other words, is "acceptable" because in our hopeless desperation, anything resembling arousal is sadly regarded as "acceptable". We lie to ourselves because more than 3 or 4 minutes seldom happens (even three or four minutes is unusual enough). So, men should feel good about themselves, even as they fail. There's a plan.

"Acceptable" suggests that the standard female response elicited regarding engaging in coitus as time moves on will be "I'm busy (with something more interesting)" with increasing frequency throughout a lifetime. "Acceptable" means the slow wearing away of a relationship. But, it's "acceptable" because that is the best the stupid humans can expect.

Everybody should be lasting as long as they please and making coitus a desirable, not tolerable, experience. Desirable should be standard procedure in so many ways. The woman saying, rather, "That sounds like fun!" throughout a lifetime.

Ten minutes or so has to be exceedingly rare under today's (unassisted) conditions. I say that for many reasons.

It's just ludicrous to survey men for two minute performance when the woman needs 10 minutes *unless* failure is so common that no one wants to admit it is a problem. "It's just the way it is." "We're only human." Please, take a survey if that makes you feel better.

I began my whole search a decade ago by desperately scanning the web for some way to extend the experience as I finally began to realize the source of our madness. There is *never any* suggestion that men can last ten minutes, much less until the lady sings. Like most men, I was convinced I'd find something. Just look at all the webpages!

Nothing. The answers range from "If you work at it, you may last 2 to 3 minutes" to "give it up, use cunnilingus, a dildo, or change your stripes" (great backup plans that do not fully usher in our sentient state).

All of the answers regarding how to last even a few minutes involves disrupting the flow or the experience, one way or another. They are all an animal's answers. *All* of the answers assume that it will be over soon.

One of the most amusing and common suggestions is, "think about baseball" rather than loving the woman. Right. There's a plan that highlights how much loving is currently involved in the man's effort. It becomes a narcissistic effort rather than an effort to love the woman. He has to take his mind *off* of loving in order to attempt to succeed at loving the woman. Incredible.

Indefinitely delayed ejaculation is not even a consideration. As far as I can tell, the term has never even been used before. It is the requirement that has never even been considered and the only one that answers.

In other words, in the current environment of the distorted, disrupted, dysfunctional human condition, if you are a man, good luck. You're on your own at the bewildering age of mid-teens with zero valid information available. After that, it's all downhill. You will learn to accept and embrace all of the nonsense and misery in desperation. That last sentence is true for everyone, not just men.

So, let's make it clear. Find some way to fulfill the woman's sexual desires until humanity can find the natural way in which a man can last indefinitely. No more bandying around the situation. No more avoiding the woman's needs.

How do you think a man must feel when he fails his own expectations regarding something that is such a big part of being human and one's daily life? It is repeated endlessly. How is it that he can fail at loving a woman in a thoroughly human, loving, sentient way??? It derails a man's mind. Some convince themselves, they are only animals. Others just hide away. None (or very few) truly succeed.

If any truly succeed, they need to make known how they do so (if they even know).

Can you see how this failure has stunted men in particular, and humanity as a whole?

That you are in your mid-teens when it first destroys your world is just the icing on the cake.

The misery hits below the belt. There's probably no one with whom to feel comfortable discussing the failure (this is also true of both genders), so you ache in the misery that you don't even admit to yourself.

At this point in our journey as a species, a parent can't help because they know nothing. So, you are on your own. No one is going to pull you aside and even say, "It's broken", much less provide resolution.

Good luck but don't expect too much out of life. Or, as one common phrase puts it, "Life sucks and, then, you die." That should be enshrined as the epitaph of a failed humanity. It is time to rise, like a Phoenix, from that failure.

The question of how many, exactly, are lousy at sex is not even worth discussing. The generally accepted estimate is 30% to 75% can't last two minutes.

Keep a few things in mind.

Two minutes isn't even a good start.

It starts from a base of 100% that have to learn something more than an animal in order to last more than a few seconds to a minute.

Ten minutes isn't on anyone's radar as far as I can tell.

It is near certainty that if the question were rephrased as "how many can last indefinitely" the answer would be zero or close enough to it.

Yeah, we cope, right? But, do we really? Do you really see any improvement in humanity over the millennia?

Why in the world would a perceptive, intelligent race just cope with unsatisfactory results from coitus? What else could blind us to our animal antics and, worse yet, revel in them? How could a highly perceptive, intelligent race not find a way to overcome such an obstacle to its fulfillment? How can we continue to act like an animal and deny the potential existence of fulfillment? Can you not see how we have been fumbling, hiding and deluding ourselves since the beginning? Like an animal.

It enrages me that we invented the little blue pill instead. It is so screwed up it is beyond belief and implies so much about our aborted sentience state, our human condition.

All of the distorted, bizarre, absurd, ludicrous conditions that we tolerate can be laid at the feet of humanity never transforming the act of coitus into a human, loving endeavor. All of the distorted, bizarre, absurd, ludicrous conditions started with our distorted, bizarre, absurd, ludicrous views regarding coitus and sex, in general. We still perceive with the perspective of an animal. Can you imagine what human life will be like when *all* of humanity knows how to love, rather than just half?

In all of the ways in which we try to mimic the fulfillment of eye to eye coitus, there is not a single one that transforms sex into something singularly human. Eye to eye, unassisted, mutually satisfying coitus is exclusively human. It is the goal.

Our current attitude is that all of the aberrancies of humanity are natural occurrences. If all that was in store for us was being a smart animal, I would agree. That seems to be the consensus today. We are no better than the animals. Just more intelligent and, therefore, far more dangerous to everything we encounter including ourselves.

I beg to differ. Nature knew what it was doing when it created a highly sentient race. It's high time humanity does also.

The ideas rattling around in humanity's head regarding the finer qualities (e.g. honour, integrity, etc) of being human never seem to get any closer.

A discussion of the problem, its importance to the human race, various alternatives and how to achieve the ultimate goal of loving coitus needs to become the most prominent topic of the Great Conversation of humanity as a whole. Just the admission that women have the right to sexual fulfillment would go a long ways towards resolving our insanity and women's inequitable position.

The ongoing struggle to express those finer qualities reveals that there's something more that nature has in store for a species that can do all of which we are capable; a race that can sense concepts like love, honesty, honour, integrity, grace, generosity, responsibility, sensitivity; a race that over and over again tries to look behind the curtain with no success. The wizard is us. Let's get on with it.

You really think we are currently on a path that makes the slightest sense? That is fulfilling? Or, are you just coping and contending with the situation as best you can? Waiting patiently for it to be over?

We have to face the fact that, so far, we have been horrible at loving.

A change of state

Once men can show their love in the most natural way, their love will become natural and their emotional upheaval will disappear.

A male animal's duration and that required by a female in order for her to achieve climax are not consistent *without* human, sentient intervention. We never seriously attempted to intervene.

The simplicity of a man achieving human, loving resolution to the difficulty is so obvious that it becomes clear we have been avoiding the consideration at all cost *because* it is an unmitigated disaster.

This becomes eminently clear if one considers the inaccurate term, premature ejaculation. For an animal (which humanity is), it is the *norm* for males to last a few seconds. So, why in the world do we use the term "premature" when a man does it? And, declare two minutes success when a woman requires more like six to fifteen minutes??!!?!?

The idea that a few seconds is premature but a couple or three minutes is success puts the whole situation out of kilter. It implies that there is nothing to be done in order to please a woman during coitus - the stance we have held for millennia. Hold on and hope for the best.

Premature ejaculation (in fact, everything regarding ejaculation) is "baffling" to the researchers. They never mention men learning how to last long enough to make it into an act of love. Instead, women are supposed to accept men's failure and placate the man's ego. Right. Look how that's working out.

Studies suggest that 30% to 75% of men have difficulty lasting more than *two minutes*.

The inescapable conclusion, since two minutes is accepted for men and a quarter of an hour is the requirement for women, is that there is no expectation that women should achieve orgasm during coitus. They must just tolerate men's failure and, worse yet, for the religiously delusional, never even attempt to achieve orgasm in any other way.

There are also studies that ask women if they experience orgasm regularly or ever during unassisted coitus. They reinforce the conclusion. The studies range from 60% to 75% of the women say no. I continue to be certain it is closer to 100%. It is our great loss that we have ignored the situation.

Nature provided and humanity ignored. Men can last as long as the woman pleases.

Think of it this way. We tinker with everything in order to improve it. Why in the world would we ignore this disaster? It is the first and foremost crucial fear of failure.

We have ignored a situation that throws our sentience into upheaval for some very complicated reasons. It is disorienting as long as we ignore it. It is destructive. It doesn't need to remain that way.

Until the discrepancy is addressed in a *human, sentient* manner, our human nature remains unfulfilled. As long as we lie to ourselves about the situation, we remain less than an animal.

Men can learn to *act* like a human but that is not the same as *being* human. It is only going through the motions. The *act* is played out in the Theater Of The Absurd.

Men take and women give. It begins in bed. Not because it is a man's desire to fail at loving a woman.

It is only because we surrendered to failure long ago and created the coverup of all time. That surrender compromised our humanity and created the delusions in which we exist.

That surrender is so unlike humanity as to make it stand out like a neon sign. It is a big deal. The obfuscation sealed the deal for three thousand years.

What makes it such a stupendous mistake is that coitus can be completely transformed. There is no reason that men can't last until the woman is pleasured. It's ridiculous to even consider that men cannot find a way to last long enough without any foolish assistance other than his brain.

The confusion is deep and abiding. The wikipedia article and all of the "research" and "studies" on sex make that clear.

The ongoing confusion and disorientation wrecks any chance of humanity attaining a sentient perspective. Sentient awareness seeks truth, clarity. What happens to that sentience when it is deliberately deceived?

My guess is it is closer to 100% of men that don't perform than anyone cares to admit.

It's a big deal. It is bad enough that men remain lousy at coitus. The big, big deal is the deceit this has caused to emerge and flourish in the heart of humanity. Deceit is not human nature. It is part of the human condition.

Our human nature entails far more than just reciprocity of pleasure during coitus, of course. Loving coitus only begins the journey into a fulfilled sentient state. The missing element of loving coitus, and the deceit it engendered, causes the calamity in our midst and voids our human nature.

Why is there such bewilderment about the situation? One phrase that is often encountered when researching the concept of premature ejaculation is, "the exact cause of premature ejaculation isn't known." That is purely ridiculous.

The more appropriate suggestion is that premature ejaculation is a legacy of the animal that we need to and can overcome.

How do we overcome the *animal* condition of uncontrolled ejaculation (rather than the false depiction of premature)? That begins to open the door. The answer is that we apply our sentient intelligence to the problem.

The real question then becomes how does a human male overcome a limitation that animals have always endured without a second thought?

We start with a human definition of what is desired: "indefinitely delayed ejaculation". When the man consistently exceeds the desires of the woman, we become human. I like that sentence a lot. There is a load of double entendres in that statement that suit the sentient situation.

Since we are not just animals (not even "merely human"), the situation begins to clarify.

We are still acting like an animal when we say just "try harder" or "hope for the best". "I think I can, I think I can, I think I can" is not enough. That is an animal attempting to *act* like a human. It makes it into an Olympic event when we just "try harder". That is the dimwitted beast ringing in our ears.

Do you think men could possibly be okay with not satisfying their lover as they know damn well should be possible? No matter how much we attempt to blur the issue, our sentient awareness remains: it is essential, and should be possible, to love a woman physically. Our repeated failure to make it so and the accompanying deceit regresses us to an animal's point of view or a disoriented human view.

Do you now understand why so many men have difficulty with the terms, love and make love? We are not natural liars. Men have been forced to lie about the sexual experience due to the juggernaut of history, delusions and circumstance. That many despise the term making love makes that clear. They know it is not yet so. Just another example of the inherent honesty (desire for clarity) of humanity, even though our clarity was undermined long ago.

It's a shame because humanity would be in a lot better shape if we just admitted to the situation and accepted that women have every right to find ways in which to achieve orgasm until men find their way.

The *human* goal is to satisfy one's lover. It is only the ultimate goal to take coitus as it was given to us by the animal and transform it into the fulfilling experience that only a human can comprehend and desire.

If you wish to comprehend the most essential difference between the genders, take a moment to ponder that women have *always* satisfied their lover.

The ultimate human goal (for both genders) is to look one's lover in the eyes as *they* achieve orgasm, the most transcendent experience possible in life, and thus feel fulfillment. The train never leaves the station for a man. The ultimate is when it is true for both the man and the woman.

Do you now see the defining difference between man and woman? It affects everything regarding the two genders? Many of the traits attributed to being female are, in fact, nothing less than the attributes of a human that is not hampered in its humanity.

By their very nature, women make love. Men need a little sentient intervention in order to do so. I have provided a lot of the insight necessary to make that true. You are welcome.

The current thinking seems to go that we should be able to think ourselves into a blissful state of existence, no matter how disappointing everything regarding the human experience is (all due to this single debacle).

We've tried *that* for thousands of years. Look where it has gotten us. Even if we could meditate ourselves into our navels, it is no substitute for the outpouring of love that should be expected from the human race.

We hide as best we can from the situation but, being sentient, it is unavoidable. Something is missing from sex for a human, sentient race. When you look around at the disarrayed human condition, you are looking at the fallout of that unachieved potential.

It's easy to understand how early humans might wish to return to being a dumb animal. They were faced with what seemed an impossible task. Making it all go away might have initially seemed very attractive. We have followed that foolishness for *three thousand years* or more.

Anomalies

Any way you look at it, men wanting to condone lasting two minutes during coitus, while women need more like six to fifteen minutes is peculiar. It just doesn't add up unless something is very broken. Men know they are disappointing women.

Try as hard as he might, the man knows the woman requires a lot more. That has been dawning on humanity forever, but we didn't want to hear it. Yeah, that worked well.

All that was required was the realization of how important it is. It is critical to get it out in the open in order to do anything about it. One half of the human race cannot succeed at that which makes life fulfilling. Instead, he is left with only his own pleasure and a gaping hole in his existence. We all know it. We all carry it around like a bomb ready to go off. It is time to admit it and address it.

Do you really think that gazing into the eyes of a lover and failing to express one's love physically can do anything but make a person miserable, utterly destroy their humanity? Especially when the human race cannot even admit it?

There are so many similar anomalies when it comes to human life.   Let me provide one from personal experience. I know others have had the same experience. It all gets so bad, on occasion, that I just had to laugh.

While I won't get into it, the human condition is filled with just such anomalies, absurdities.

The span of loving

A span of a few minutes should not be called premature ejaculation, it should be called standard procedure for any animal. If a human term should exist, it is unassisted (pills will never make a man) indefinitely delayed ejaculation.   That is what is desired and required by a sentient race.

The *key insight* is that there is *absolutely no reason* at all that a man has to *start* the ejaculation process while aroused and engaged in coitus. Rather than fighting against the tide of the coming ejaculation, just don't start the process until the desired end is in sight.

The proof is everywhere but we don't want to look. I guess it just confused us. We have inadvertently ignored every insight that answers the question. I mean, how baffled must we be to never consider that when, errrr, "practicing", he has difficulty reaching climax? Why does a man have difficulty in starting ejaculation during "practice sessions" but, when with a woman it is all but over before it is ever begun? I've heard some way, "it's different". Duh.

Worst of all, is that a man learns to do all the wrong things during "practice sessions" that make sure he ejaculates quickly. That such habits spill over into his attempts at love-making is no surprise.

Unleashed from the paradigms of nonsense and forced obfuscation, we can redirect our inventive and creative sentient nature in order to overcome this bane on mankind. The animal, basically, does some really stupid things. But, then again, it's just an animal.

All of our absurd antics regarding sex are due to our stunted attempts to make coitus human and loving.

Finding the joker in the deck that has been there, unobserved, for more than three thousand years has been the struggle of humanity up until this point in time. It just takes a little serious thinking to begin to clarify.

Sentient resolution is achieved through an altogether different approach from struggling to last a few moments longer. The goal is to last until the woman says, "enough". If one realizes that ejaculation should should not begin *until it is desired*, it becomes a different question that can be answered.

Men don't attempt to last longer just due to a desire to last longer. Men attempt to last longer to sexually satisfy their lover. Two to four minutes is not nearly enough and, deep down, everybody knows it.

The false premise emphasizes that we not only remain an animal but a demented, confused one at that. At the very heart of our existence, we have deluded ourselves. All of the nonsense we cooked up to avoid the realization is really choice stuff. I'm sure our descendants will be rolling in the aisles with laughter.

We have effectively isolated the issue, the situation, from reason. Lasting longer is not a goal, in and of itself. Tell me it's not strange that we have so confused the issue.

The gaping hole in our sentient existence is due to avoiding our sentient awareness that coitus can be far more than any animal ever imagined.

Tell me it's not special that a human can gaze into the eyes of their lover during the act of coitus. I don't know about you, but I can't think of a more fulfilling way to fuse love. This is more than unusual for any other animal.

Instead, we turn out the lights. Tell me that's not strange.

Our inability to achieve such a crucial goal as transforming coitus into a loving physical act devastates an advanced thinking, feeling, sensual, emotional being. Hiding from the conclusion and not accepting alternatives until it is so is the death knell on a sentient perspective.

Could it be that looking into the eyes of one's lover awakened something in early humanity? We are the only animal to be able to do it, other than the bonobo monkey, which is altogether one strange beast when it comes to sex. We turn out the lights?

Love can only truly blossom when coitus contains the human element: mutual transcendent pleasure. Indefinitely delayed ejaculation is just a precondition for that to occur. Once men can feel content that they can love a woman physically, their human, noble characteristics can begin to emerge. They can begin to be human and loving.

If humanity could just accept that it is crucial for a man to find a way to provide sexual satisfaction to their mate in some way (other than a pill) would be a huge step forward.

Not much to say about the real characteristics that we will learn to call masculine. It won't be anything like the buffoonery we countenance today.

Seeking fulfillment

Men have always attempted to avoid *the final step* in the process of ejaculation. They have attempted to "choke off" the flow *after* it has already started. That is where humanity's effort to make coitus a loving event began to fail miserably and led to the erroneous term of premature ejaculation. How long can a man hold on?!!?

Because of this debacle, men still tell themselves that the best that they can expect is a few minutes. Right.

Lessons from history

Here's what happens if you rely on "experts", "authorities" to arrive at answers (have I mentioned I'm not fond of the terms?). It is the basis for all of our paradigms of nonsense.

I choose this one, in particular, because of its ancient history, as well as its subject matter. The *Kama Sutra*, which is like a bible for sex, was first created around 2,000 years ago. It was the original sex education. Real sex education, not just lessons in the dangers and horrors of sex. It was way too involved and complicated to become commonly accepted.

The author, Vatsyayana Mallananaga, declares that he wrote *Kama Sutra* after meditating on ancient books on the subject of coitus.

It never entered Mallananaga's mind to consider that a man might just be able to last as long as he pleases because he relied on "experts" from the past. They didn't consider it, so he didn't consider it. Ad infinitum, right on down the line through history to today.

I do not mean to denigrate the *Kama Sutra*. It may be the finest book ever written regarding coitus. The poor sod did a fine job of attempting to make coitus something other than the normal animal interaction. It's just way too complicated.

The problem is that such complications seems to freak people out a lot. "You mean I've got to work at it?" No, I don't and that's the point.

The *Kama Sutra* is like a form of romance, making coitus into a work of art, like dancing. Okay, the rigamarole could get annoying but, hey!, at least they tried. Instead of saying, "Ugh. Me man." They said, "I like women enough to try to do something about it." Even if it was overall a bust, they tried. Me, three thousand years later is pretty pissed that someone didn't follow up and break through a long time ago. Like before I was born.

All of the rigamarole in the *Kama Sutra* is unnecessary once humanity learns how easy it is to engage in loving coitus. It is far better than the bovine instruction of, "just stick it in" and, maybe, "hold on for all your worth". But, still, *Kama Sutra* was way too difficult, too complicated.

I love what Timothy Taylor has to say in his book *The History of Sex: Four million Years of Human Sexual Culture,* "The idea that there is a sexual line (of conduct) that must not be crossed but, in practice often is, is far older than the story of Eve's temptation by the serpent." There's a lot packed into that statement.

There's really only one thing to be learned from the history of sex. We haven't learned a damn thing. We sensed there was something more but fell flat on our faces (yeah, I'm really enjoying this).

We have mesmerized ourselves by repeating the mantra that "we are only human" and coitus doesn't work. Awwww.

Just like the more noble qualities of humanity, we have never attained the finest quality of sex that can only be created by a sentient race.

One huge difference between the finer results of coitus and the nobler qualities of humanity is that we just abandoned the former as hopeless. The latter, we keep dreaming about and wonder why we can never attain them, while simultaneously drowning in the delusions that cause us to look away from their source. Training Pavlov's Dog to *act* human is the best we've come up with, so far.

Mutual satisfaction through coitus has never been taken seriously. It's just not the way coitus has ever worked, even for millions of years before humanity ever arrived on the scene. So, we disastrously shrugged our shoulders and moved on. Big mistake.

All societies, all cultures are inured to men lasting a very few minutes. We are also inured to tolerating all of their bullshit that men have created in its absence.

Conundrum

Sentience has allowed us to upgrade everything about life, except sex and, thus, our humanity. We've improved our toys, but humanity itself is just as messed up as it ever was while scratching its ass in a cave, maybe worse. We have hemmed and hawed for three millennia. We are no closer to attaining our human nature because we never suspected that coitus is tied up in creating a human, sentient, loving version of humanity.

We separated the act from its loving results. Sex is just sex. Right. Rutting is *not* loving. We convinced ourselves that the lack of the loving results of coitus has nothing to do with the inability of humans to provide and experience loving emotions. While I believe that accepting the situation until it is righted and finding other ways to fulfill the woman's physical desires is a huge step forward, loving coitus without assistance is the ultimate goal. It may very well be that it will take some time to achieve the ultimate goal, so accepting any alternative other than manufactured manhood (i.e. the pill) may be crucial in order for us to step away from the edge of the cliff.

When it comes to anything regarding the subject of sex, our mindset exceeds absurdity. We just accept the animal's premise and stumble along creating inadequate, and often offensive, alternatives and excuses. Offensive alternatives are those that resort to violence in any form. The rest of the alternatives are just inadequate substitutes. Better than absence or abstinence but still substitutes.

Sex remains just as we found it. The only thing our creative faculties have consistently added to the sexual landscape is perversions, delusions, and excuses. At these, we have exceeded all expectations.

Sex plays such a central role in our existence that the ensuing confusion and deceit infiltrates every aspect of the human narrative. That shouldn't surprise anyone, though it probably will.

It is a fundamental desire of a *human* to achieve mutual sexual satisfaction and, thus, love. The icing on the top is gazing into the lover's eyes during the transcendent experience. It completes the circle. The poor men have been banging their heads against the wall for that answer forever. Now, we have pills. Great. Thanks a lot. We remain an animal.

The bizarre behaviours of men that have baffled women for ages can all be put down to the failure of making coitus into something human.

Do men wish to be good at sex? Ya think? The little blue pill proves the case, as well as many, many, many other oddities of the human condition (porn industry, sex "therapy", I could go on all day).

I mention all of that in case it is not intuitively obvious to you that all men wish to be good at coitus and, thus, achieve a loving, caring, rational, emotionally balanced state (though they would never admit it today). Instead, men quickly become ensnared in the delusions promulgated by failure and the surety that there is nothing to be done. Just act like everything is okay. Don't panic!

Mutually satisfying coitus has never been taken as a serious possibility. Our brains usually go haywire regarding sex, especially during sex, especially during orgasm. This may be the reason it has taken us three thousand years after we began to develop our human narrative. It is like the simultaneity of failure and orgasm just shunted all thoughts on the subject aside.

This also clearly fits in with the current human confusion, narrative, and condition. The *condition* is that men are bad at coitus from a human, sentient perspective. The confusing *narrative* that we all accept is that men *aren't* bad at sex. Everything is just fine. After all, they can last two minutes! Just look at all the satisfied women in movies, romance novels, and other fictions. Do you begin to see the insanity of it all? Many, many must believe the problem is just them.

The confusion and deceit is rampant regarding sex. Since it is such a crucial and constant presence in the life of a human, the confusion runs rampant through every other aspect of our existence.

Sex is so fundamental, so essential, to the human, sentient narrative that everything remains broken, animal-like until the narrative of sex becomes human and rational. It is the fundamental deceit that opened the door for the rest of the deceit that continues to rain down on us.

A man's confidence and self-respect are worn away as he achieves puberty and fumbles through repeated failure. The remarkable justifications that go through a man's mind, the furtive desperate efforts to hide from the truth, are astonishing. Sadly, miserably, helplessly, and hopelessly, we have gotten used to a bad idea. Worse yet, we have not whole-heartedly accepted loving alternatives (e.g. dildoes).

Alternative resolution

Keep in mind, the most fundamental problem is the distortions to our sentient environment caused by the confusion and deceit that we have maintained regarding sex. That is far worse than the actual sexual failure and our inept inability to repair the situation.

Humanity will not change in any significant way until human consciousness accepts that human, loving sex is radically different from that of an animal. Human, sentient, mutually satisfying sex begins to create a loving state of mind for both participants. It makes us human and distinguishes us from the animal with no confusion, no impetus to return to the animal state.

The term "make love" is not frivolous. It is just that it has been relegated to describing just about any form of sex, even those in which the woman never achieves orgasm. Rutting does not create love. By the way, it is the only form of sex in which the woman does not achieve orgasm.

Lift-off

Why have we not avidly pursued resolution regarding something so fundamental? It is clear that we know it is important. The studies, efforts, and other gibberish are endless. The importance is underlined every time we turn out the lights, take a little blue pill, or search the millions of useless web entries on how to last longer.

The importance is emphasized each time we address the nonsense of the human condition with further nonsense. Every time we attempt to address the human condition with nonsense, we just erode our sentient perspective further.

While it is not a straightforward insight to discover what is not working for a man, it is not so difficult as to have taken us more than three thousand years to figure it out. I figured out most of the essentials in about three years, once I pulled back the curtain and rid myself of all of our delusions.

Furthermore, while it is not a straightforward insight, it is a straightforward effort. I've taken care of the former. The actual effort required, once the insight is understood, is minimal. It is on the level of learning to walk. It just introduces a minor amount of forethought into the male consciousness and takes a little time and discipline to overcome the instinctual efforts of the animal. Once it becomes common, our "instincts" will change. Remember those two words: forethought and discipline.

We remain convinced it is impossible, so we soft-sell the whole experiential disaster and write off our humanity.

Why does the subject of coitus and sex, in general, remain a distasteful subject? It is because we know we have not yet gotten it right and wish to avoid the subject at all cost. We should be celebrating it.

Making the woman's sexual satisfaction an imperative, however it is achieved, removes the obscurity and absurdity that have been pulled over the human race's consciousness since the beginning as we followed the sexual antics of the animals before us.

It is the prerequisite for the final fulfillment of the human concept of love and our human nature. The fulfilled mental state of a sentient being fulfills the attributes of love, stabilizes the emotions and provides for our humanity. Loving coitus is the further achievement of a sentient race that accepts its awareness rather than running from it.

Self-respect and self-confidence are shattered on the rocks of our failures to achieve mutual sexual satisfaction. They cannot be replaced by mantras or training Pavlov's Dog. Without sentient, loving sex, we remain little more than a really smart and very dangerous animal. Our self-respect and confidence are missing. What we see in their absence is an act and a poor one, at that.

Humanity has the potential for an advanced form of caring that we term love. It has been mostly incapacitated by our inability to learn to celebrate its most powerful, transcendent, transformative physical aspect.

The utterly distorted state of sex creates the nasty carousel of nightmares that are the result of our determination to avoid the subject.

A man figures out in about two seconds that he's not very good at coitus. He either seeks lesser alternatives or bashes his way through and accepts failure. It takes him another forty years or so (if ever) to admit it to himself or create excuses for his lack or substitution. In the meantime, it erodes his humanity in limitless ways.

I can't really say how women feel about it, though disillusionment and bewilderment seem the common reaction to the offensive behaviour of men, if not the failure in bed.

Not surprisingly, women tend to get furious at men. Not so much for being lousy at coitus but because they are lousy at being human. Men don't want to admit what is really wrong and, arguably, it never even crosses a woman's mind.

We lie to ourselves constantly regarding the subject of coitus. "I'm too tired" or some other deceit is used to cover up the truth (by both genders) as they age. The bickering of couples is no surprise at all.

Our current views on love are a jumble of nonsense inspired by the failure to make coitus into a loving engagement: women desire love and men desire only sex. Now, why do you think that is believed to be true? The inhuman narrative accepts this as the essential truth, rather than the state of an animal. You better believe that all men begin with the desire for love. It is just crushed out of them. And, we want humanity to love all??!? when we can't even love a single other person thoroughly?

Indefinitely delayed ejaculation is like walking on two legs. It is something every human male should be able to do. It is the key that unlocks the door to a sentient fulfillment.

It needs to become the common expectation and utter shock should be expected when a man does *not* succeed.

Achieving physical manifestation of love makes us human. It transforms the human race. Love is not as mystical, ephemeral, and unattainable as we make it out to be. All of our other knowledge and accomplishments mean nothing without it.

Yes, many men will be embarrassed in the short term. But, think on this. That has been the case for *many* millennia.

Human Consciousness

Human consciousness, the sentient state; which includes heightened awareness, intellect, curiosity, creativity and imagination; is a progressive state in which we become more attuned to the universe that we inhabit by exploring and inspecting it much more closely than any species before us (curiosity, awareness, intellect) and manipulating it to serve our purposes (creativity and imagination).

Be crucially aware that the manipulation that furthers our efforts at clarity and sufficiency is far different than the manipulation of the truth into lies and nonsense to cover our failure at becoming human. We have excelled at the latter when it comes to humanity itself. That has only destroyed any attempts at clarity.

Our heightened awareness has been assaulted by creative misdirections regarding sex all through our long emergence into sentience. Our human consciousness has been blunted into the stupour of an animal.

Curiosity, in the form of self-inspection, was abandoned long ago, thus it turned outwards. In other words, the species has no real desire to look in the mirror. In the absence of self-inspection and revelation, creativity and imagination turned towards destruction, starting with self-destruction and moving outwards.

We have missed the most important realization until now. While we have improved our understanding of all that is around us, we have yet to understand humanity itself. We don't look inwards with curiosity due to the ingrained fear of what we may find. What we *will* find is our humanity, if we are honest with ourselves.

We have avoided a close inspection of human nature versus the human condition because it raises some uncomfortable questions that were only uncomfortable because sentience was once new on the scene and coitus was an old reliable. How could our earliest ancestors have conceived that there could be something more to sex? How could old reliable be so unreliable?

Make no mistake, all of the most important realizations required in order to make humanity whole have to do with humanity itself, not its constructs (e.g. governments, corporations, religions). The constructs of humanity are where we have concentrated every bit of our efforts for improvement. Not humanity itself. We abandoned the mirror.

Human consciousness is filled in by the narrative that we tell ourselves. The more widespread any particular narrative becomes, the more it becomes a part of human consciousness. The closer that narrative comes to matching reality, the more fulfilled humanity becomes.

Just think about it. Lies have always made us uncomfortable. Just picture that feeling on a grander scale, the scale of humanity. The same rules apply. We have been lying to ourselves for a very long time. It is so embedded that we hardly think of it as lying.

We are seekers of truth and clarity. All of our delusions regarding sex, particularly coitus, undermine any attempt at clarity regarding the human condition. Since the beginning of rational thought, reason has been denied when it comes to sex. Regarding coitus, it has been explicitly unreason.

Humanity is a potentially noble race, even though there is nothing particularly noble about the current human condition. We know it. We have attempted to become a noble race, over and over again. In fact, we are so adamant in our belief that humanity *can* be so much more that it shows up regularly throughout history. But, it never became part of the most common human narrative. Our search for clarity knows better. We are not there yet.

Every attempt by humanity to achieve nobility has been crushed. Something stops us cold, sooner or later, every time. The animal finally rebels against those attempts to *act* human in the absence of that which makes us human.

There are few that even make the attempt to become noble any longer. The famous and celebrated people you so admire nowadays require a much closer inspection. The whole human condition requires a *much* closer inspection.

To put it succinctly, that is the difference between the human condition and human nature. Our current situation is due to our current faulty human narrative that creates and maintains the human condition that is not really human at all. The narrative is built on paradigms of nonsense and the animal that must be abandoned. Nonsense and absurdity have nothing to do with the sentient, loving race we can be.

Humanity's consciousness must realize that humanity can be a loving race and how to do so.

The distortions chip away at every one of us as we achieve physically maturity. The feeling is, "something is wrong with this picture." We desperately seek some way to comprehend what is wrong, while wildly thrashing about to avoid any close inspection of the coital situation, only to finally succumb by saying, "That's just the way it is." After all, "we are only human".

The most emphatic example of the feeling that something is wrong, in recent history, was The Flower Power Generation. A large portion of a generation had a vague idea of what needed to change, so they screamed for something to be done about it and proposed the false narrative of "Free Love" as a solution They finally succumbed by saying, "that's just the way it is" (just ask Smashmouth).

The same completely crushing admission has broken the human spirit, over and over again, generation by generation, throughout history.

We *know* in our hearts that something is wrong but we can't quite put our finger on it. We know that it shouldn't take thousands of years to evolve into something more than a demented animal.

We know all of the offensive characteristics of the male human that has yet to become a human, a man. So far, we have just accepted them as "just the way they are." Do you hear me screaming in frustration?

Even though the interpretation of "Free Love" (as "free sex") was way off base, it brought us so much closer to the realization of the linkage between coitus and love. The words said it but the actions refuted it. In our most insightful, inspirational moments as a species, throughout history, we have sensed what is wrong but could never quite put our finger on it. We have to face the truth.

What happens every time is that we end up looking away in disgust (due to our exasperating conditioning) as we accept that coitus is not what is seems rather than accepting that the real problem is our inability to make something more of coitus, something human. "Sex is cursed!" is one of the favorite cries of the inquisitors. "It is heresy to think that any sex is good!" is another. We fight tooth and nail to even admit that there is something wrong with the human adaptation of coitus (due to the same exasperating conditioning into delusions).

This is about an intelligent species coming to grips with an incongruity. The incongruity is caused by our sentient awareness of the animalistic circumstances of coitus that do not fit into a sentient perspective while any discussions on the subject are shut down, with prejudice. We have avoided inspecting closely the primary situation necessary to achieve our humanity. Amazing!

There are no good solutions to any of the many problems that humanity creates - until we become human. All of our attempts result in gibberish as long as we continue to flounder. We attack surface issues and ignore the heart of our problems.

Do we clamp down on hate speech or do we regale each other with the importance of free speech? Neither works. If you suppress foul speech, the foul utterances just goes underground. If you allow it, the most foul utterances of hate and insanity are proclaimed openly by brute animals. Does everybody carry a gun or nobody? Neither makes us human or furthers the cause of humanity. Okay, fewer guns would keep a *lot* more people alive, at least in the U.S. but it still doesn't make us human. Less guns and suppression of hateful views would just make us appear a little bit less of a deranged animal. It changes nothing of significance.

Don't even get me started on the insanity of Incel and Red Pill (speaking of hate speech, insanity, and the failure of loving coitus). If anything, they just highlight the road we are on as long as we remained convinced that men must remain lousy at coitus. They proclaim it a man's right to have sex with a woman whether the woman desires it or not. Rape by any other name. So, so very sick.

All attempts remain gibberish until we become human. Our thoughts will remain too chaotic as long as the incongruity regarding coitus remains hidden in our midsts (just ask Incel members).

Humanity remains a demented animal because it has not accepted its responsibility as a sentient race. We become bitter at the realization and start shooting each other. There's a plan.

Once we become human, *then* the problems begin to fade because they are mostly problems of a demented animal. The problem isn't free speech versus hate speech. It is that hate, rising from self-hatred, exists. It is that hate is accepted as a human construct. It is *not* government and all the rest of the human constructs that are broken. Humanity is.

Sometimes, that sense that something is deeply wrong flares up like a beacon, as was the case with the Flower Power Generation. But, still we continued to struggle to pin down exactly what is wrong. We end up popularizing each flare of outrage of youthful exuberance and innocence as childish rather than a real sense that something is wrong. As the soul gets worn away, we accept "that's just the way it is."

That "youthful" exuberance and innocence should last a lifetime. They are not the problem.

All of the thrashing about we do is done by poor actors playing out their folly on the stage of the Theater Of The Absurd. I could never accept that we are nothing more than fools on a stage.

There is one single, essential, tangible, crucial circumstance whose ramifications must be addressed before we can ever achieve our humanity.

In case you missed the point, that is leveling the playing field of sexual gratification, leading to the ultimate goal of loving coitus. It's a big deal.

Sentience begins

This answer, this truth, is required for humanity to gain an unobstructed sentient perspective. Until the human narrative changes to include loving sex, we will never even begin to know what it means to be human or have a thorough understanding of what love is, not to mention rationality, sanity, and stable emotions.

Coitus, today, is a failure for the human race. It is just fine for the animal.

Loving coitus must become part of humanity's consciousness. It should drive us on until it is fully attained. The lack of even the consideration of mutual gratification as a necessity leaves humanity out in the cold. Our consciousness must become unfettered.

By unfettered, I mean a view or perspective that does not *purposely* blur reality by concocting nonsense in order to hide our failure. The only other choice is to remain an animal.

Without all of the enforced delusions, like "Life sucks and then you die" or "We're only human", we can finally acknowledge that sentience is truly different and should be fulfilling. We will also finally realize that this existence, for a sentient race, need not be a disappointing cockup.

It is *not* rational to wait for some distant, vague point in the future that will never arrive. Some distant point at which humanity will rise above its mess due to keeping the nose to the grindstone is just another delusion. We are not just an animal and it starts right now.

We have gotten so used to creating delusions and deceptions, whole industries have been created out of it (think snake-oil salesmen and extrapolate).

Success

We don't have to just put up with unfortunate circumstances, like an animal. We change the rules of the game regularly through the good offices of our sentience. Yet, coitus remains the act of an animal, even though we know something is missing. We have trained ourselves to just look away. Lie about it all, if necessary.

Coitus remains the unspeakable. Rather than take a hard look at coitus, we chase a myriad of ways in which to achieve the same result. I don't know whether it is hopelessness, stupidity, or just the training. All that is clear is that we gave up on coitus long ago.

The fulfillment of the physical act of coitus that transforms it into something human creates a human mindset in which human love can finally flourish. Do you understand that? Do you get that? It is really important. There is no other way for humanity to get there, to end the arms race between the genders. Mutual gratification in any form would declare a truce and may succeed in making us human. But, the fulfillment of loving coitus cannot be overstated.

Some of the sexual alternatives seek the same goal, love through mutual satisfaction. Why is it that the one for which humanity was made remains a failure. Instead of acknowledging the one in which we can gaze into the eyes of our lover in complete joy and transcendence, we look away.

It is dead easy for *humanity* (and only humanity) to change the narrative regarding sex. All it takes is men finally learning to perform adequately at the sexual act as a human should. All of the delusions will fall like dominoes.

I've been pondering the thought that a lot of our confusion originated in the short-circuiting of the brain that seems to happen during sex, especially during climax. How is anyone supposed to think straight regarding the subject of sex when the brain goes on the fritz during climax? Or, the woman's case, when it ends all too abruptly in mid-stride. I'd guess the latter would be pretty baffling.

After the act, most attempt to put the failure out of their minds, make less of it than it really is. Going immediately to sleep works for some.

The narrative

Just keep reminding yourself throughout all of this book that I am not suggesting changing one or two men's mind, or even a hundred, or millions. It is only unleashing humanity's conscious awareness and clarity by changing the narrative of humanity that will suffice.

The mutual gratification of human, loving, fulfilling coitus frees us from a burden we have always carried, causing misery and pain all along the way. Mutually gratifying coitus is the seed from which love grows. Without it, love withers on the vine, at best becoming a shadow of itself.

We can only become human once this is fully understood *by the human race's state of consciousness*. The human narrative must reflect that coitus and love are intertwined in the human act of mutual gratification.

Do you really believe heinous acts would be carried out by full-fledged humans that weren't an emotional shambles of irrational reactions? Do you begin to see how failed coitus causes those reactions? Do you really believe that those that enact heinous acts are the only ones that are broken by the miserable state of sex? Do you really believe that laws fundamentally change anything? It is a long drawn out process that goes nowhere. It is whackamole. It is an animal's reaction.

Can you not see how all of the confusion, deceit, and delusions (i.e. misinformation served up on a platter) are created by our sexual conundrum? That the sexual mire creates *everything* disturbing about the human condition?

Men retaining their self-respect, retaining their confidence in themselves and their sexuality, would produce a far different gender. That transformation would, of course, relieve the feminine gender of many burdens.

Today, perversions are the rule, not the exception. They are a confusing escape mechanism from the failure.

Until today, there has been nothing to be done about it. In that shattered self-respect lies all of the perversions, the absence of noble human qualities, and all of our self-produced troubles.

The noble qualities of humanity cannot be legislated. They cannot be recovered by training or mantras. They exist in the human spirt, in human nature. They have just been crushed until now.

In stupefaction, fear, and certainty of failure, we never broach the subject. Only as our growing sentient comprehension forces our awareness of the situation, do we react. Our intelligence and awareness were initially caught unawares, blind-sided.

Whether success is assured or impossible, we still have to confront the truth in order to provide clarity. Coitus is a mess and the inability to face the failure has spawned confusion, delusion, and deceit.

Creativity regarding sex has reigned unhindered by awareness or intelligence. As long as awareness of the truth is hindered, our humanity remains buried.

For me, there is something special, something particularly human, about gazing into the eyes of my lover while achieving mutual gratification within her. I cannot accept any other alternative. Any of the broken alternatives do not suffice. It is why I tried so hard to figure out what was broken regarding coitus. Success is not nearly as crucial as accepting that we are currently failing to make coitus something that a *human* desires.

I am certain we can succeed at loving coitus. Everything indicates that Nature has provided the way. I hope dearly that I have provided that solution or the beginnings of that solution but, no matter. Once humanity trains its focus on loving coitus, it will be. Whether my feeble attempts address the issue or not, we will desire to bring it to the form of high art. Loving is a form of high art. It may be the essence of high art. There is a lot of evidence to suggest that is so.

Seeking closure

All of the offenses that I may seem to lay at the feet of men, really needs to be laid at the feet of circumstances. I am certain that in our current finger-pointing, all-about-me condition, some people will want someone to blame. There is really nothing to blame other than circumstances. It is just a matter of sentient evolution. Men were the unwitting victims (thus, making women the unwitting victims, as well) of the worst catastrophe that is the natural (and horrible) result of becoming a sentient race from a sexual animal until we slowly evolve into our sentience and accept clarity.

That is the first step. I do believe, to take the next step and fulfill our loving potential, we must make coitus an unassisted loving success. I dearly hope that the two coincide. No matter what, though, we must at least face the facts and deal with them, however we can. I just have a hard time believing humanity cannot make an unassisted loving success out of coitus. I've done everything I can to make the two coincide. I hope it is enough to get the ball rolling.

While I tend to adore women, partly because they are much more sentient than men at this time, I am becoming annoyed by one particular anomaly. I have had conversations with a number of women on these subjects and I found that many do not want to let men off the hook.

They reject all of this out of hand. They do not want to listen. I guess that is understandable for a number of reasons but it does not further the cause of gaining our humanity. The two genders acting like armed camps does not get us anywhere. It will destroy us. Excusing men for the failure does no better. There is only one way through.

We evolved from animals for which coitus was nothing but rutting. As humans, we have accepted an animal's act in embarrassment, bewilderment, and shame. We have concocted the most insane rationalizations in order to avoid facing the issue directly.

If you don't believe the following statement, then you are from a different planet than me: *everyone is seeking love.* We want love so desperately but it invariably ends up, at best, a pale shadow of itself. Many, then, proclaim love a fiction or a lesser definition is accepted.

We become human when we accept a narrative that stands up to our conscious awareness. To say it another way, our conscious awareness becomes human, when we are no longer trying to fool ourselves. Another way to say it is we are seeking clarity.

Love

I can't put it any simpler than this. Successful human, sentient, loving coitus creates human, sentient love. Now, I will take the next few paragraphs to explain that which is so utterly simple to say.

Essentially, only love can distinguish humanity with certainty from all other animals. We seem to have realized that for a very long time. It's a sentient thing. Sure, animals care but not on the level that humanity can attain. It is something new. It is Nature performing at its finest.

In some amazing way, nature provided for a state in which a sentient being can step beyond all of its past. That is the essence of sentience. It can see the incongruity and change it. More than a butterfly from a caterpillar, we can transcend the genetics and inertia of a lesser existence.

Nature provided a way to completely bypass the animal antics to get to the heart of the matter. Love. That really blows me away.

Love cannot thrive in the environs of the animal. Love cannot fully succeed without loving coitus.

In the beginning, there was a sentient race that was as uninformed as a bag of hammers. The race grew up accepting that which had come before. Sex was nothing more than rutting.

As their intellect and curiosity grew, they began to wonder if there couldn't be something more to sex. Maybe women should share equally in that incredible feeling of orgasm during coitus?

These insights was dashed on the rocks of their inability to do anything about it and, thus, the myths like Pandora's Box and, then, The Garden Of Eden were created. The former was an attempt to explain a baffling realization. The latter was an attempt to divert blame. The riddle, not surprisingly, completely baffled our ancient ancestors.

Instead, they concocted strange proclamations, like sex is only for making babies. Sex is cursed. If you have sex just for fun, there is something wrong with you. If you want both participants to enjoy the experience, there is something wrong with you. Etc, etc. etc.

The transition is striking. The wonder of human life was quickly replaced with finger-pointing, excuses, and blame. I am sure there will be some that will be horrified by the idea that coitus can work well for humans. But, then again, they get horrified a lot. Heck, they are horrified by humanity.

The fact is that half of the human race is running around with its self-respect in tatters and substitutes ludicrous behaviour in a failed attempt to correct the situation. Some survive the lack relatively unscathed. Others completely indulge their lack of self-respect. Humanity is not yet human.

Yes, most endure, but why should we endure the absence of that which can make us astoundingly human?

Male *animals* take and female *animals* give.   Human, *sentient* males give as well as take. So far, few or none exist.

One example of the confusion is the common belief that men's desire for sex is the problem. It is just another example of shifting blame. Self-respect is not toppled by a desire for sex. It is toppled by the inability to make sex into something human and, thus become human and retain one's self-respect.

Because we had no clue that anything *could* change, we initially opted for animal rutting. It was necessary for the human race to continue to procreate and, thereby, continue to exist. It is time to change.   Our awareness has been becoming more and more frustrated as time goes on and our awareness of the sexual situation evolves.

Unlike an animal, the lack of success at mutually gratifying coitus crosses a human's mind.   In fact, it lodges there and burrows deep over a lifetime. The narrative needs to change to fit the facts.

Until a race can think about coitus seriously and openly, it cannot do something about it.   We essentially blinded our awareness regarding this topic, then we proceeded to run around like a bull in a china shop.

I am a paradigm-breaker. It's what I do. And, yet, due to all of the garbage we are fed from the moment we are born, it took me most of forty years to break through the bizarre set of paradigms that we all accept and, finally, break them to pieces. Layer by layer, I stripped away the facade until the real culprit was exposed.

It should be clear to you by now that there is no reason that coitus should be any less than what you always dreamed and imagined. I hope my insights get us closer to that fulfillment of our humanity.

The worst part is not the failure itself.   The worst part is never confronting the fact in open discussion. We continue to run around bewildered by it all.

Take the leap and try to make coitus into something human. Men must learn to give as well as take in bed.   Eye to eye through the whole incredible experience is best. That begins something more tremendous that you may imagine. It will transform the race.

Populate the planet with humans, rather than animals mimicking the human state, and the great majority of problems *caused by humanity* will end.

Just look around. How many of our problems are caused by humanity? The aberrant behaviour of humanity causes the bulk of our problems. The aberrant behaviour lies in the disparity between that which we perceive versus that which we admit.

Fulfilling our human nature separates us definitively from the animal. It is permanent and decisive. Realizing (and admitting) what is missing is the first step.

When only half of the race knows how to give and love, that is just the witless extension of the animal condition.

Half of our race has always been prone to giving - in bed and elsewhere. It is *their* tentative sentience that has gotten us this far, against all of the bestial background noise. That's all that has kept us from tearing ourselves apart over the last three thousand years, though we have tried as hard as possible and are probably getting very close to reaching that goal, if we don't become human soon.

Truth is a beautiful thing

Seeking truth, reality, and, thus, clarity is difficult, even without the convoluted delusions and nonsense created and directed at denying and avoiding the truth at all cost. To say it drove us insane is understatement.

It has taken me four books to get to this point of clarity. That surprises me less and less. The truth is so difficult to grasp that it has taken me ten years to begin to see through it all to the point that I can express it clearly to some extent, even once I arrived at the heart of the matter.

My efforts were impeded by the paradigm defenses we all carry around that are developed in order to avoid the one single, complex truth that derails our humanity. It is so intertwined in our existence that it is very difficult to unravel.

That's fine. Once we expose the real problem, accept that pills and other alternatives are only a distraction, not a solution, we will succeed.

I guess I should thank all of those that read the previous books and still couldn't get a clue. Because of that, I had to keep clarifying. Naw, I'm not going to thank readers for being obtuse. I was fine with my intuitive understanding. I was not fine with the outpouring of nonsense I received in return. I am just giving it one last try. This is clear enough.

Nature provided the promise in a lover's eyes. It also provided an elegant and simple means by which to fulfill that promise.

It's not like it takes a PhD in order for a man to be good at coitus. A simpleton can do it. With self-respect and confidence retained, there will be far fewer simpletons.

The man must now learn to focus on the woman rather than desperately propping up his threatened manhood and male ego in the most ludicrous manner while continuing to fail. He must learn to overcome that which causes the feeling of shame and brokenness in order to show his love physically. He must quit being preoccupied by the fact that "he's only human" and become human.

<u>Lies and all</u>

Can you believe it? It took me more than a decade to recover enough to even begin to discuss this in a coherent enough manner to have the slightest chance of conveying the situation to a race of beings that has been geared to accept lies. While I will remain tentative about the results of my insights, the insights are certain: we can become human.

The deeper I study this, the more shocked I become. Men have been lying to themselves for thousands of years and everyone else has been complicit in the lie.

What a cockup! It is to be expected but, still, what a cockup! Men, of course, didn't do it intentionally. They just woke up one day with this realization that women should have climaxes during coitus and were at a complete loss as to how to make it so. That was thousands of years ago. We are a different humanity now. We can succeed.

It was easier for our witless but highly creative and inventive ancient forefathers to invent a completely fictitious existence, in which we remain bound, rather than admit there was a problem. We lied to ourselves to cover up the false truth that there was nothing to be done.

It was just the way coitus worked. So be it. Let's not discuss it at all. We made any mention of coitus or the dilemma off limits. That is a very strange reaction for a race that strives and thrives by improving everything.

We have remained in stasis ever since. Men lied to themselves and everyone around them because there was no other alternative for the simple minds at the time. Our minds, our awareness, our existence are no longer simple. It's time to put the animal behind us.

The deceits became part of humanity's narrative. It has gone unchecked for, at least, three thousand years. Deceit developed right alongside mankind. Intentional, self-serving deceit ends when we become human.

Do you think it's just happenstance that we so easily deny anything regarding reality that doesn't suit each individual's singularly distorted perspective? Does the phrase, "perception is reality" begin to offend you utterly as an offense to our human nature?

Offensive arguments

As a man, I hate the idea of being the one that _always_ ends incomplete sexual congress. Don't you? That sucks. Talk about undemocratic! I want another vote!

Can you imagine, as you lay there within your woman saying, "Anytime you're ready, love." It is breathtaking to contemplate those words. It changes everything regarding being a man. It creates a man out of an animal.

Can you imagine anything better than face to face, eye to eye (open eyes, that is), mutual, simultaneous (or thereabouts) orgasmic coitus? How often have you achieved it? How did you opt out?

I basically had to check out for about four decades, while I chipped away at the nonsense we all bought, hook, line, and sinker.

All of that time, it was like looking down the barrel of my misery and failure as a man, still missing the point that it is the unimproved state of many men, if not all. Once that latter point began to sink in, all of the curious behaviours of humanity and especially men, immediately crystallized.

The litany of lies

I don't know if I really want to start a list. It would be endless but, still, it is tempting. The whole human condition is a fictitious representation of a human, sentient existence. In every way, our existence should be expected to change for the better.

We are currently living an animal's interpretation of what sentience should be like. It is so distorted that it becomes extremely difficult to figure it all out.

Is there anything that is not a fiction? Besides the misery.

We have been on this endless loop of deception. You might as well consider damn near anything you encounter as suspect. The more blindly you are devoted to a concept, the more likely it is a foolish lie in which to hide.

This and that

This chapter is like a throw bag in which I tossed pieces that seemed to have no particular home but were pertinent to the discussion at hand (or monologue, I guess I should say, sadly). Each new topic is preceded by a dash. This and That makes it seem like I am digressing less. ;~j

You have to understand. I surveyed everything for forty years. Instances of interaction that just didn't make sense and, of course, there were a lot of them. Then, add it contemplating our bizarre history, cultures, organizations, and religious beliefs developed over three millennia. That's a lot of moving parts. All of which I was juggling around trying to fit into a sensible scenario, like fitting pieces into a jigsaw puzzle. Or, finding the answer to a riddle that evolved over three millennia.

Then, it hit me like a ton of bricks. It was hiding in plain sight because it had been so obscured by the bizarre effect that coitus caused in an animal that evolved into a being that could see the flaw. It was hard to detect, at first, for a sentient race. Coitus had always worked well for animals, so why should it be different for humanity. The prehumans did everything they could to avoid the issue.

That meant clamping down on thoughts. While it was directed at the curious case of coitus, it eventually clamped down on thought across the board.

Anyways, as I said, it made for a complex picture. That is why I have written so many books on the subject and I could write another fifty trying to explain it all.

These snippets help condense a lot of it. But, there is still a lot that is contained in each of the books.

- This chapter, also, could have easily been titled, Thinking Out Loud.
- It's not like this is all about sex. If anything, it becomes much, much less about sex once we get coitus right.

Look around, we are *obsessed* about sex *because* coitus hasn't ever worked right for humanity.

Once coitus works as humans have always expected, it becomes less about sex. It becomes much, much, much more about love, life, the overall workings of humanity, and functioning like an emotionally balanced human race living in reality. It is time to do so.

- I've mentioned often how many feel that the failure is a rare occurrence that only they endure. That has compounded the confusion. This makes sense in the light of the truth. We tend to believe that any human should be able to make love because any human *should* be able to make love.

- It amuses me that some sexual orientation rights activist don't think that heterosexuals should have the right to have good coitus. Political correctness at its finest.

- It has been difficult for me to see past all of the offenses of men to the heart of the matter.

We grew up as a sentient race with a heightened degree of awareness but zero knowledge. This intense level of confusion and distraction led to an offensive level of deceit.

It spread in exactly that manner. It started as confusion, led to distraction, and finally evolved into deceit as a way to distract in the case of the very pressing issue that wasn't so pressing when we first evolved into a state of sentient consciousness. We readily accepted the failure of an animal existence, which is not a failure for an animal but is surely a failure for a sentient being.

We could pick away at so many confusing subjects but some became nearly insurmountably camouflaged by deceit. The closer it came to the great deceit, the more desperate the distraction became.

As I look at it from this perspective, I think I begin to see clearly what a frustrating existence it would have been for the poor saps. They were burdened with a horrific growing realization regarding the act of coitus with not enough information to deal with the subject adequately. Considering that it involved humanity's ongoing existence in the form of procreation, it must have been a horrible, desperate feeling. The best they could think of was distract from the issue. Man, did we screw that one up!

I have to believe that, once we do away with the clutter, once and for all, our minds are going to free up in a way that is difficult to describe. Every thought today needs to be processed, not just for information, emotion, and/or content (e.g. imagery, etc), but also for honesty, truth. That is the 90% I keep talking about.

Deceit should not be an overriding concern for a sentient race that accepts reality and deals with it. What a mess! Maybe that is why any time I see purposeful misinformation of any kind (yeah, including diplomacy and statehood) I see red. Call it opinions, but it is nothing more than deceit. Appallingly, offensive deceit meant to distract us from a highly intelligent and fully aware existence. All because ... well, that's what these books are all about.

Most of what we have seen down through the ages are the worst characteristics of men due to their feelings of inadequacy. I have focused on this a great deal.

It is a lot easier to describe today's Keystone Cops version of masculinity than the eruption of male humanity into something human, which we have yet to see.

We've seen the lovely characteristics of women, even though they have been hampered by the situation. We've also seen the awful characteristics that the results of the situation. Their fine qualities have been seen down through the ages, even while compromised by the situation. Can you imagine a day when men also show their humanity?

The most difficult challenge regarding women is separating out those characteristics that are human and those that are feminine. Many characteristics that are classified as feminine are only so because men show them seldom. Toxic masculinity will never admit they are human characteristics since toxic masculinity has never portrayed them.

What is much more difficult to determine is the *new* characteristics that men will make evident.

But, I don't think I'll get into that, other than to mention forethought, discipline, and romance, once again.

Maybe more than anything, this is about men reaching their full potential and no longer cause a drag on our humanity. I try to see past all of the illusions, when it comes to men. There still remains something to be revealed. Something about men becoming fully human that has not yet been seen.

Once the toxicity of men is stripped away, there will be some aspects of love that will remain unique to each gender.

Then, I think of the true fusion of man and woman into one. I could say words like equality, etc and maybe that's what it will be all about. The fusion of man and woman into one will also create something new.

The future will reveal all of this, so I won't make any conscious effort to do so.

- Do some folks fear that men becoming good at coitus will break us? Look around. We are broken. Loving coitus is the only remediation. Or, do they fear the failure will not go away. If that is the case, just shoot me. We are done.

- It seems like we are entering the final stage of the fiasco we have forced on ourselves. It's impossible for us to remain just an animal. We are too well equipped to play the mindless animal game of survival of the fittest. The end game for humanity, along that route, is a dead end, literally. We must assure that love creates the human.

It can't turn out well for an advance life form that clings to its animal legacy. We are too well equipped for destruction as long as we remain only an animal.

Life, as a human, is about so much more than just surviving. Today, the most ruthless are considered the strongest. That is an animal's perspective that does not work for the more highly developed sentient state of humanity. Our desire for truth and clarity will never rest. Without it, it seems certain ruthlessness will rule and destroy us.

- There is nothing we can't do. We have shown that in every facet of life except loving. We succeed at so much and fail at loving.

- Even if what I suggest to make coitus work right doesn't work for everyone or perfectly, if we open up about it, we will find a way. It's crucial. Pills will never make us human. In this one instance, we really need to do it ourselves. No outside support.

We have to stand on our own.

The paltry remains of love that we squeeze out of life is nothing like the glory that a sentient race can attain.

-    It really makes me want to cry, once again. Humanity really has to come to grips with the horrible human conditions created by men's inability to learn to love.

I would just bet there are some out there that believe that a loving, caring, sensitive attitude is not manly. That is nothing more than an animal's perspective, which makes sense. If that is the best we can do, just shoot me.

Keep in mind that men have been trained for a very long time to be as they are. All of those foolish characteristics come from attempting to cover up their failure for millennia.

Think of how paranoid, bitter, or dismayed a man could become thinking every other man is better than him in the very real, very worrisome reality that he is lousy at coitus.

Now, fast forward to the current situation. While there are plenty of people (not just men) that are beginning to realize that it really is many men that are messed up (yes, regarding coitus but even more than that, being human).   That does not lead anywhere good unless it changes.

-    Does it not seem highly significant that men's character is so undermined that the overall reaction of the gender is to lash out at women? From micro-aggressions to macro-abuses towards women (and all of humanity, nature, and existence), men have shown that they have not yet become human.

Can no one see what a debacle this is? Can no one see the fundamental cause of all of this upheaval?

Can no one see that the preponderance of violence against women (along with so many other offensive traits) are nothing more than the actions of a cornered animal?   Heck, I am sceptical that anyone really even sees the true pervasiveness of the violence (especially against women). Can no one see that the animal needs to become human in order to finally end the nonsense?

The micro-aggressions show that training and laws will never change anything. The instability is within the individual man and is not removed by proclamations or producing feelings of guilt and shame or prison sentences or capital punishment. As long as we all continue to lie to ourselves, nothing really changes. As long as we cannot face what disturbs us, we lose.

Human consciousness must evolve to take into account the coital situation in order for humanity to become human.

The offenses just go underground, otherwise, where they become unchecked and considerably more dangerous. That is always the case. That is why we seek free speech and, yet, it never really works. Rules and training lead nowhere.

I'll admit, I am not too fond of what we call education, either. We teach how to learn, not how to think. I would expect that will change, also.

- What makes you so sure there needs to be human misery? That is the other myth I have never bought.

Basically, we remain a stunted race, attempting to fill the sentient shoes that Nature provided and, so far, have failed.

We have never really tried. We were alway afraid to take a good hard look at what is wrong and attempt to do something about it because we were so sure we would find only an abyss. We've danced around the truth since the beginning. Instead, we curse our sentient state and watch it continue to fill with misery.

- Don't even give me that drivel about "it's a rough world out there". *We* make it that way! It's not the world that's rough. It is *humanity's condition*, not humanity itself, that is rough.

Human nature is not. We have yet to fill the shoes of the sentient race called humanity.

- Can men be trained to *act* like humans. Sure. A person can learn the right responses to seem human. Makes me think of *Stepford Wives*. Then, I think of lying, cheating, humans. They are not human.

Being trained to act human is nothing more than a monkey in a suit. The suit never fits. It is just foolish, incompetent *actors* prancing around on the stage of the Theater Of The Absurd.

- It isn't like men woke up one day and said to themselves, "Let's go give women a hard time." No. Something stirred that tumult. Something caused men's emotions and sentient life to go haywire.

The offensive behaviour has a reason to exist, it has a source. It is like a thorn in the paw. Women have tried to tolerate the roaring behaviour and alleviate and ameliorate the pain. But, the situation that causes pain must be eliminated in order for men to become self-respecting, confident humans.

"Pulling oneself up by one's bootstraps" does not make for a loving human. It makes for a mindless, irritable robot, unless that bootstrap pulling also involves learning to love.

I know how hard it will be for women to comprehend. They don't experience the failure but only see the results. Their baffled reaction to men's antics proves the case. It's difficult enough to get men to confront. Women don't even have a template to understand the failure.

All of the mannerisms of men are affected by that feeling of failure. How they interact with other men and with women is driven by that failure. Everything about the male gender is driven by the failure.

I just don't know how to better explain the effect success or failure at such a seemingly natural aspect of existing as a sentient being has on a man. It is night and day. It is human or animal.

The more I think about it, the more I am amazed. How do we not see this? If we do, why haven't we addressed it?

Basically, nature did not care about bringing balance to the sexual pleasure of an animal. Its only intent was to reproduce. Mutual gratification would have just confused the poor beast.

Humanity, as an animal with heightened awareness, is far different. Humanity was made to distinguish the truth, always seeking clarity.

The truth is there is a missing element to human coitus. Clarity is provided when we finally admit it. Our humanity is provided for once we overcome the obstacle.

An animal's enactment of coitus is not complete. There is an element missing with which a witless animal could not be trusted. More importantly, a human can fulfill that missing element. We must. We are far more than an animal ... or can be.

Coitus was made in a particular way in order for animals to survive. We outgrew that, as animals recently promoted to the status of sentience, millennia ago. Comprehending all of this that was beyond the grasp of the animal, especially how to make coitus into a loving fulfillment, is crucial.

Look around anywhere you please. We dance around the subject of most importance and never admit that men do not please women sexually. We lie to ourselves and act like there's nothing wrong.

Shouldn't coitus be complete, fulfilling? Why would we tolerate the situation for three thousand years, unless it scared us spit-less and witless. We run around finding alternatives rather than resolving the issue in its natural setting.

We have the wherewithal to improve our situation. We are not the witless humans that first encountered the realization. Avoiding the issue had nothing to do with our inability to improve it. It was all due to the inertia that came from the animal.

Men must be more. That's about the best summation at which I can arrive. There is something limiting and cringe-worthy about accepting that men cannot become successful natural lovers and, thus, fully human. It's utterly insane. So is continuing to hide from the failure. It drives men insane and destroys the human condition.

-    Maybe later generations, as they can begin to view this all in retrospect, will be able to nail it down better. I have been compromised by living a life in the midst of all of the delusions. I just hope I have been clear enough.

For now, maybe the best description is that the act of fulfilling coitus creates lovingkindness. It is an act of lovingkindness. Self-serving rutting is the act of an animal and never reaches lovingkindness.

-    We treat love as if it were some fleeting thing. It is becoming common for people to expect love between man and woman to dry up and blow away in short order (e.g. failed marriages and miserable ongoing relationships endured). We run away from the failure into the arms of another ... and another ... and another, alway seeking fulfillment.

It would be more appropriate if we thought of love as a state of mind that can only be retained by retaining one's self-respect and confidence.

-    It is about so much more than just the love between a couple. It is about humanity fulfilling its role as a sentient race.

\-   Think of it this way. What else in the universe can possibly substitute for the love of another? Loving another without self-doubt, hesitation, inhibition, guilt, shame, or constraint initiates a loving state of mind. The failure to make coitus loving causes the failure of a loving state of mind.

Instead, we take the racing heartbeat, feelings of lust and confuse it all down to an irreducible minimum of what we consider love to really be all about. What a crock.

\-   It's not like we can drag ourselves up by our bootstraps and just declare ourselves human and loving. That is what we have always attempted. How's that working out for you?

It takes the fulfillment of the physical act of love.   For animals, there is no such thing. For animals, it is no more than sexual relief. The only way to change it into an act of love is for the act of coitus to become fulfilled and fulfilling.   The act is transformed when the satisfaction is mutual and we can finally open our eyes.

It is about emotional stabilization and the ability to finally convince ourselves that being human in something more than being smart and destructive. Even admitting there is currently a problem will go far towards stabilizing our emotional condition. It might even be enough to make us human. It seems unlikely to do more than that.

Once we really become fully human and accept without question what sentience provides, all bets are off.   We will become something that I'm not sure anyone today could even begin imagine.

\-   It's just staggering to realize how terribly mixed up we have been. The deeper I go, the more blown away I am.

For instance, the way each gender interprets the actions of the other gender is so amazingly wrong.

Of course, it all started with men requiring that the great secret was never revealed. It confused us beyond measure.

Because of that single necessity, everything was warped away from true.

An example is the whole misconception that men have no need for love. I mean, really, think about it. Men *learn* to do without love after breaking it repeatedly. You are terribly deceived if you think men do not initially seek and desire love.

The first proclamation of love by a young man is, for most, an honest interest. Then, the failure comes home to roost and it falls apart. They learn to use love to get sex only because that is the best they can do.

Now, consider a generation that grows up without the bane of failure. It will be something to see.

I think I've already covered men's horrible reactions and perceptions towards women under our current circumstances. The reactions are not pretty at all.

As the self-confident and self-respecting young seek love, it will be with eyes wide open as they celebrate the moment. Finally.

It's not about the words. You can spout about love all day long if it is not confirmed in the loving act. It's about the actions that confirm love in the heart of the one that acts.

Men only take and women only give in bed. There lies all of our problems. Any alternative in which a man gives in bed is a big step forward. Loving coitus is the final conclusion that answers all.

Any man that does not seek their lover's satisfaction in some form should be considered pariah.

Love's Survival

Maybe a more positive way to look at it is that it is about love's survival. In most cases, an individual's love for others is trampled over a lifetime. It would be nice to think that some few people's love flourishes over a lifetime. I think not, not *flourishes*.

The cycle of renewal comes to mind, again. Each generation is a new source for the emergence and survival of love. It can flourish in a heartbeat. Our sentient awareness is not going away. Our delusions only need to lapse for love to flourish.

Allowing love to flourish is the next evolutionary step.

And equality

Maybe another way to look at it rather than the difference between training men and men becoming human naturally is this.

Do you think it would be better if men weren't dragged into treating women as equals? Do you think that an equality between the sexes that is begrudgingly granted because women howled loud enough and long enough can hold a candle to equality that is attained with open arms by both genders?

It freaked me out when I thought back on my two wives. Each one did two things I never understood, until now.

This first one is the one that really threw me for a loop. They would do something wrong (break a rear-view mirror in one case) and, then, cringe, like I was going to lambast them or something. I mean, what the hell, right? Many women have been trained to cringe. It's an outrage.

The other one still baffles me. Both told me that, if I wanted to fool around that was fine, just keep it hidden. I was utterly disappointed and baffled. Disappointing one woman at a time was always enough for me.

Bits and Pieces and a new language

- Why do you think so many turn to another person, besides their lover? Why do people have affairs? It's been so hard for me to put it into words that anyone can understand. But, now, it makes sense at an even deeper level that I think, just maybe, makes sense and can be understood.

The confidence and self-respect implicit in being a loving being is compromised by failed coitus. The failure also implies that there is no love, that honour has not been met. A man feels that he has already betrayed his lover through his failure, so what does it matter if he steps out? The woman feels betrayed, so why not step out?

Funny thing. The woman doesn't feel nearly as betrayed by the lousy coitus as the emotional vacuum that it causes in the man. Crazy.

- There is one particular song that entranced me, as so many of a particular artist's songs do. It is such a mixture of fury and tears that it put me into an even deeper state of ache regarding this horrible excuse for an existence that is ***not human***. And, there goes the fury to match the ache.

Further evidence of the failure of our humanity and its source is contained in the lyrical catalogue of so many artists. The boundless expectations of love in youth slowly transforms into the bitter dregs of accusations and frustrations regarding the dismal results. Or, an endless, churning array of relationships.

Some of the most lovely music all dedicated to a memorial service for love. Of course, mostly by women.

It just hurts deeply to hear these songs that sense the ache and the boundaries of the problem as they are experienced with no sense of what the real, underlying problem is. I hope that changes soon. I cannot wait to hear songs about love consummated, fulfilled, and spreading across the Earth.

- Later in this book (and elsewhere), I talk about how this discovery required that I create something like a new language.

I think it may be important to consider this. Don't expect any of this to come too easily. It will take a great deal of effort to initially put away the worst of the delusional paradigms as an individual and as the human race. Whether we get there or not will depend on how many individuals are willing to make the effort to understand and pass it on, in the form of these books or their own words and commitment.

I so look forward to an existence in which all of the miserable aches of failing love, compromised love, faithful observance of the rules - even in the face of the utterly failed prospect of love - all become a thing of the past.

- That sense of love is an outgrowth of our inherent sentient state, our human nature. That is what breaks in men when faced with the failure of coitus. The transformative aspect of a sentient existence that unleashes love has been denied them. It all feels like a cruel delusion/deception when the most intimate act of love fails.

The shared physical love, in the form of mutual coital satisfaction, transcends and fulfills our intuitively inherent sense of love.

Loving coitus makes it more than just a vague sense.   It makes it real, tangible.

- I have tears and fury in my eyes as I, once again, look at how hard we try to become human and repeatedly fail. I used to think that I was just crying for myself but, now, I finally realize I am crying for humanity.   How do we put up with this shit? (Answer: Frog in hot water).

We try so hard and, yet, never get anywhere.   The abuse continues, the micro and macro-aggressions continue, the misery continues, the suffering continues, the insanity continues, the misunderstandings continue as we remain only an animal.

Much more so, the inequality and lies continue.   I am not just talking about the horrible and otherwise unexplainable inequality between man and woman, in this case.

The real traitor that has betrayed us all is one particular deceit.   We deceived ourselves concerning the most important aspect of being human and, thus, learned to lie and remained nothing more than an animal.

I don't know which is worse. My tears for our attempts or my fury at the useless stupour that remains, the pompous certainty of fools. Of course, there are offensive people around! We aren't human yet!

- Don't you get it??!?!   There is no grindstone except the fiction of one that we stuck our nose into rather than look up at the seemingly awful truth that is not truth.   It is nothing more than a deceit!

- We don't *need* to remain a combative race!   The combativeness is what has been hardest for me to ever comprehend.   Whenever faced with combativeness, I was baffled.   I never understood it.   It is such a useless exercise ***between humans***.

- We talk about freedom a lot. We don't even know what true independence is all about. What do you really think binds you so tightly that we talk of freedom? From what exactly do we desire liberation?   We need to be liberated from the lie that distorts our sentient clarity, the animal. That's all.

-    Pull out one of the props which have been used to distract from the awkward elephant in the room that no one wants to talk about and watch the curtain fall behind which it hides.

I think about the wonders of this life that go by the wayside because everyone is so caught up enacting nonsense that it leaves me aghast.

The more that my double vision becomes focused on the future and begins to let the present fiascoes take second place in my mind, the more aghast I become.   Our missing potential makes me ache with awe for what could be.

I think about the complications of life that could stand some really rational thought - for humanity as well as the individual - without all of the bias and blurred thinking of Pavlov's Dog and it infuriates me. There's no reason for all of the nonsense. Sigh.

-    What really gets me is the constant (believe me or check history: it is *constant!*) outrage at our circumstances combined with the unwillingness to look for true resolution.   We just accept it all like lemmings rushing over the cliff into the sea. The one's that jut their jaw out and stubbornly say, "it's just the way it is" make me utterly sick.

-    What is really beginning to blow my mind is that the thought of *improving* coitus to suit a human environment seems to repel most everyone so thoroughly that they won't even consider it. That's some deep delusions powering that.

The rationalizations to justify one's own compromises with coitus explains so very much.   I had those same quaking thoughts when I first encountered the missing nail but I had already assembled all of the dots which instantly made it all clear, even though the words to explain were a decade away.

My own horrible experiences of failure just nailed it all home.

("Missing nail" references an analogy from *Sentience* regarding this whole mess.)

-    What do yo think will happen when you think about sex seriously? Do you think some god will strike you down? With all of the offensive, destructive, and outright vicious nonsense that your gods have ignored, I wouldn't worry about that.

- Does it make you furious that men might actually become human? Do you want to hold a grudge against men, even as humanity comes crashing down around you?
- Why is sex considered cursed by so many? Why do so many violent perversions of sex exist? These are no small questions and all of the answers have been inadequate (by which I mean non-existent), until now. We look on in horror and acceptance as we say, "that's just the way it is."

The only answer that has even been suggested up until now is that we are just animals. I don't disagree. I only add, "so far". The dull-witted acceptance of the situation is that of an animal.

Redirect all of those questions regarding our failure to become a respectable representation of sentience. Direct them at coitus remaining no more than an animal's rut.

- The University of Chicago wrote about a study that showed that nature made a remarkable number of genetic changes in order to result in the human brain.

They suggest that it might have been because of the evolution of social order (I am more and more convinced that looking into the eyes of our lover during coitus (or closing them) has a lot to do with it).

I know this is going to sound pure crazy but it sure seems to me that looking into the eyes of your lover could stir changes in the brain. Looking into the eyes of someone you care about, while failing, could certainly stir the thought that something is not right and a desire to make it right. Every time we don't, the animal wins. The desperate desire to look into those eyes while not failing could stir a lot of thought. It did for me. A lot of thought and confusion.

Due to the fulfillment of loving coitus, all social interactions will improve. Our current less-than-human sex life taints everything regarding our humanity and our interactions. It is corrosive.

The tone of interaction will change drastically over time as we access sentient fulfillment and remove the constant irritant of failed coitus.

- The tremendous confluence of events that led to this point, this state in which humanity sees the light, as well as the love in the eyes of their lover, becomes more and more clear.

Just a few of those events were women seeking to define love, men seeking to end the horrible feeling that something is wrong while avoiding facing the issue, youth *knowing* that something is wrong and, finally, abandoning the search as they age. Each generation picked everything apart with no hope of piecing it all back together. It is truly amazing.

- We have always focused on the individual transgressions of individual human beings, never attempting to see the big picture. This is one of the points that I never, ever could buy.

We pick apart those that do not play along with the foul smell of our human condition. The human animal does not want to hear it. There is a reason that so many go insane, attempt suicide, give up in so many ways. It is (duh) because the situation is so very screwed up. "Grin and bear it", "nose to the grindstone", and such are just as offensive to me as insanity, suicide, or any other acceptance of our screwed up state. No one gets a pass, except those that finally get a clue.

- Our ancient ancestors were much more animal than human. Animals had been rutting for millions of years. That is exactly what nature had to provide for a witless species. The transition has taken three thousand years for a reason. We're talking about a tremendous change in which the biggest change is humanity's awareness, followed by that awareness realizing something is not right.

The difficulty in resolving the central issue made the simple, original humans desire to hide from it.

With the sentient human, there was created a phenomenon similar to the frog in hot water. Those earliest ancestors were familiar with the hot water of lousy coitus and totally unfamiliar with, and unprepared for, the ramifications of what their sentient awareness revealed.

We have followed that lead for far too long. It is time to grow up and become innocent. I've explained my thoughts on the bad rep that innocence has gotten elsewhere. Suffice it to say the current view of innocence is provided by, and is applicable only to, a mindless animal.

The informed innocence of a sentient being is a completely different take on life as is everything about our human nature that we have yet to fulfill.

- The lies buried below the surface of our attempts to "*act* human" become more flagrant and fragmented by the second. We have never pondered our transgressions against human awareness.

It requires more than ruthlessness and survival of the fittest for a sentient race. We don't really even ask why certain individuals transgress. We just punish them, like an animal would. Take a close look at the monkey in the mirror.

- Many point to Darwin and say, "that's just the way it is." Darwin was no more sentient than anyone else.

- Women have grown up with the belief that training men to act human, taming them into civility, will make a difference. That is understandable. It may have seemed the only option, since it seems likely women could never understand what was really going wrong for men. Even if they did, the man didn't want to hear it and remained too witless to realize they were doing it all wrong. Women have mostly given up the case as hopeless.

Self-respect cannot be trained into an individual. It is a gift of sentient existence that is lost as life progresses. Failed sentient coitus is the standard route to losing one's self-respect. I suspect, to some extent, it is standard for both genders. The traits of toxic masculinity can be viewed as the mimicking of self-respect in men. The subdued self-respect of women is closer to the sentient state due to their coital success at pleasing their sexual partner. It is only impeded by the beast in their midst.

Sentient life has to have the life-line of self-confidence and self-respect remaining intact over a lifetime in order to retain its sentience. The self-respect and confidence cannot be manufactured. Women have attempted to manufacture it for men in the absence of its natural retention by men. It doesn't work. It has probably been essential, though, to prevent humanity from yet going completely over the edge.

The more I think about it, the more I become awed by women's part in this scheme of things. Women have stepped lightly in order to allow men to keep some shred of their self-respect until the day that men could reinforce their own self-respect. That is so utterly human and sentient as to take my breath away.

- Once again, Nature's stunning scheme blows my mind. It all seems to revolve around the evolution of conscious awareness, backed by an intuitive grasp of truth, and a desperate and inexorable desire for clarity.

I spit on the phrase "perception is reality". Reality contains the word "real" for a reason. The bullshit, absurd nonsense that we have tolerated infuriates me, once again. Our perceptions are filled with delusions caused by failure.

- We are far worse off, at this point, than that poor frog in hot water. Not only do most people accept the boiling water as fait accompli, but many will justify the situation with every breath. Any suggestion that the water is hot is hotly contested.

That's what happens to a highly evolved intelligent race that remains broken and convinces itself it is only an animal.

- All of these thoughts regarding "grin and bear it", "frog in hot water", etc makes me ponder the whole idea of the numinous.

The more I think about it, it makes sense. A simple animal acquires a heightened intellect and awareness that leaves it in awe. What should it do with all of these awesome feelings of transcendence.

It knows that the awesomeness has nothing to do with its dimwitted self, so it must find some explanation for the awesome *nature* of existence.

Poof! Gods do very well for that. Dress them up and make them very, very much like a father-figure (goodness help us) and there you go.

Now, you have hinted that humanity is something more by dressing the gods up to look like humans but never have to admit to hubris.

It's really messed up.

- Sentience is awareness. Our delusions clutter that awareness into oblivion and humble us into horror.

- I can hear the imbecility now. "But it's too difficult!" or "God didn't make us that way!" or "Sex is cursed. God will strike you down for even thinking that way!" While that is what is said, the real truth that is believed, the conspiracy theory to beat all conspiracy theories is, "That's impossible."

It isn't. More than that, it is simplicity itself - for a human, once all of the lies, delusions, and paradigms of blindness are eradicated. Those are the real impediments.

- You have to first realize we are not just animals and it's not just awareness, intellect, creativity, and knowledge that differentiate us from animals.

Those, alone, are only enough to get us in trouble. Look around at what those traits produce in the absence of clarity, love, and the finer traits that are humanity's potential destiny as a sentient race.

Those four characteristics of sentience, gifted to us by Nature, just set the stage for an existence far beyond that of an animal. Until we realize that, we will remain a demented animal.

There is something more. There is something about attaining our higher ideals of love, honour, honesty, self-respect and such that transcends the animal, once and for all. It can never be a matter of sticking our toes in the water of sentience. We dive in or fail.

It is almost as if a sentient race is set up to see if it will fail to fulfill its sentient state or overcome its animal past. Do we remain an animal or become human? It is all up to us.

What Nature provided only set the stage. It is up to us to use those sentient gifts to become human.

It is not an intellectual exercise for pondering at great lengths for all time with no results. It is not something that a bright animal can accomplish through brute force.

Our sentient state seeks truth, clarity, the honest representation of reality. So far, we have hidden from the truth at the expense of our sentience. We have cowered like a dumb animal in the face of something that an animal can never comprehend. We remain an animal until we comprehend our difference.

The truth is that animal coitus is not complete. The truth is that humanity can, and must, make the act of coitus into something human, something that is far more complete than the act of the animal.

Humanity is built to seek out something better, in all ways. It is built to seek out clarity as well. So, what do you think the delusions and perversions regarding sex do to such an advanced awareness of existence and the human condition while our human nature waits in the wings?

Why is it that we fight so hard to avoid a close look at the sexual aspect of the human condition in order to realize it is broken? We act like a skittish colt. Just look at the headlines. We hem and haw but never really state the obvious.

As I move farther and farther from that state of delusion, I am horrified every time I read the obtuseness displayed in the headlines. They all say, "that's just the way it is."

Are we afraid we will quit making babies if we admit it and find no resolution? That is already happening. Birth rates are dropping like a stone.

Is it that we feel helpless and don't want to admit how broken we are? Is it that we just want it all to go away and not bother going beyond the simple animal's comprehension. Do we mostly desire to return to the simple (and stupid) nature of the animal? Do we want to continue to delude ourselves into believing all of the horrors of our existence are just fine?

We can't remain that stupid.

Inept human enactment of coitus lays low all of humanity's efforts to become human, to be more than an animal.

If one is forced to confront the issue of sex, as I am attempting to force, most retrench into their most fundamental, delusional beliefs and superstitions that were absorbed at a subconscious level since the day they were born. It makes them feel safe, I guess.

Others seem to dig their heels into the reaction embraced regarding reaching puberty and realizing it is all just a catastrophe of untold proportions. The darkness seems to claim them.

"But, we're only human!!!" Yeah, right. Maybe you are.

\- The human mind is easily manipulated, once it has been domesticated and humbled.

The deceit, the sham humanity has put itself through, is just such a humbling experience leading to domestication and, thus, becomes prey to manipulation.

I mention elsewhere how humanity, when it attains its unblemished sentience and humanity, will easily burn through the bullshit. The outrage caused by being faced with deceit (once all of the deceits are no longer conditioned into a person before their critical faculties of thinking are available) will see to that.

Think of the desire not to lie that is the basis of courts and lie detectors (that is so broken only because we remain so broken). We *always* desire truth, even in our suborned position.

Each person has the groundwork in place for clear-eyed sentient awareness, honesty, integrity, dignity, sentient innocence, and love. It is slowly crushed out of existence by the deformative years of childhood and the final coup de grâce, the stake through the heart, as pubescence emerges.

\- It shouldn't take long for humanity to recover from the awful shellacking it has taken over the many millennia. One generation with the goal in sight should be able to move mountains.

Those that seek to manipulate for their own mad, selfish reasons will fade away in short order. I hope some of them begin to perceive reality but no big deal. They will all be dead soon enough.

A generation born, without the undermining delusion that sex is just sex, should blow the doors wide open.

That does not suggest that it won't take time to rid ourselves of all of the accumulated nonsense of three millennia but, without the root cause deceit that broke everything, these others will be torn apart, sooner or later.

Things should become rather copacetic rather soon. I've always said three generations. Now, I wonder if it can be sooner. I'm probably being overly optimistic but, hey, I'm not going to be around, so might as well go down optimistic. Maybe there is more staying power to our delusions than I suspect but I don't believe it.

- Any man that can regularly last as long as his lover desires at coitus, please raise a hand. Didn't think so.

Any woman that has a man that can last as long as she *desires* at coitus, please raise a hand. Didn't think so.

Do you continue to think it is just you? You thought you were the rare exception? Just unlucky? The opposite is true. Essentially, *no one* is having mutually fulfilling coitus.

- Goodness help me, but I fear you may still be saying, "so what?"

The ideals that we once reached towards have all fallen to ashes. Oh, some still mean well but it is most rare that higher ideals are on anybody's radar any longer or remain throughout a lifetime. We are already going downhill.

- Lately, we have created pills, surgery and appliances to "improve" the situation (not to mention rape, pedophilia, porn, sadism, masochism, sex trade, domestic violence and on and on)) and we **still** don't want to admit, state *boldly*, what is really going on. None of these miserable compromises have changed anything for the better. We wallow in our misery, just as an animal would. We are only more creative, destructive, and demented.

We don't even try to figure out how men can be good at sex without assistance.

Instead, we cower in our comfort zone of nonsense picked up along the way and tell ourselves everything is alright. Really? Is that really what you believe?

Somehow, we simultaneously see the horrors of our existence and carry on with the horrors as if everything were alright. Very baffling. Boiling water.

All of the vain, vile antics that stem from men can be laid at the door of that which induces men to lose their self-respect and substitute deceitful toxic masculinity for honest self-confidence and respect.

We have built up a completely fictitious basis for our existence by ignoring something that we must overcome, something that is essential to life as a human. Something that an animal does not even consider. We threw sex under the bus in disgust and certainty of failure, instead of seeking sentient resolution.

The transition to a sentient, coherent, emotionally balanced, sane existence will happen with ease once we admit what is going on and realize we must change it all.

- Just like every sexual life form before us, we are physiologically predisposed (instincts, if you will, of the witless animal) to "get 'er done". Unlike every sexual life form before us, we have slowly become aware of the implications of just getting it done in a hurry.

All we do is turn away and act like everything is fine. Aaarrrrggghhhh!

While we know what an animal could not begin to comprehend, we avoid admitting the knowledge. We lie to ourselves because, as men thrust away with abandon, it never crosses their minds that there is another way (other than the despairing approach of "I think I can, I think I can, I think I can.").

- This all explains why the human condition in no way represents our human potential, human nature. It is right in front of us. We need not be the demented caricature that we portray every day.

- I feel like I'm still being cryptic. That is not my intent. I am trying to plainspeak something that has haunted us for, at least, many thousands of years.

It has and will continue to define our existence. It is just a matter of which definition we accept. The one in which we currently exist through which we are continuously pulled back into our bestial past. Or, the one in which we break free of our chains to the animal and attain our humanity, once and for all.

- Human brains have been conditioned to shut off the thought processes when sex is mentioned. That hampers the quality of thought processes, in general. In other words, all of our thinking has been compromised and, generally, nonexistent.

- Tell me how economics, governments, religions, economic models, or any other preposterous proposed basis for improving our predicament can possibly compare in any way to something so fundamental to our existence, something so crucial to the basis on which we live?

This is not about what we diddle around with. This goes to who we are and the detritus of the animal that we still maintain after thousands of years.

The brute force effect of laws and regulations and mores have no real effect other than to contain the madness to the slightest degree. The pressure cooker bursts apart regularly.

Those feeble efforts, so far, have never improved the situation one iota and never will. It does not get us closer to being human. It only gets us closer to making an absurd mimicry of our humanity. The caricature that I see continuing to develop appalls me in every way.

We cannot become human by relying on outside influence to force change *within* the individual through laws and other strictures. It cannot happen. The attempt to do so is an animal mimicking what it thinks it means to be human.

We are no closer to our humanity than we were three thousand years ago. It has all been mind games of imbeciles. Maybe that is another trait that has been in my favor. I have never had much use for games in any form.

Do you really think that a law should be required for a man not to rape a woman? Do you really think that little of men and humanity in general?

I know. That's just the way it's always been. Right? Sigh.

How about a man's own self-respect impeding him from such a heinous act? You can hardly even comprehend the concept, right? All of the other acts of abuse against women and a great lot of our troubles come from the same pool of men's lack of self-respect.

Sigh. I feel I have to detail the reason for men's lack of self-respect. Have I not gone through it enough? Men still act like animals because, in the act of love, they revert to the animal context of rutting rather than the human act of making love, ***and they know it***. To be more specific, to speak in a language you may understand, they know they fail. **_That_** destroys their self-respect and confidence in themselves. The human, loving act of coitus has seldom, if ever, been attained.

What came with sentience was the potential for being lovingly human, only impeded by the drag of our animal roots. Failing to make the act of sex into a human endeavor has kept us from becoming fully human.

- The final catch-22 that forced all of this: A man would rather fail at sex than do without sex. So, in defense, men built rationales that buried reality. Women were complicit. Willingly or unwillingly, I haven't a clue.

Think about it. A man's own sentient cogitations have betrayed him since the beginning. Man wants sex. Man does his best to avoid any uncomfortable thoughts that something is wrong since it seems completely unaddressable. It seemed impossible to do something about the fact that he ought to be lasting longer but, for some unknown reason, could not.

As it became more and more obvious, he railed against the situation in every way possible. Poor duped fool.

Does this explanation work any better than the previous ones I have attempted?

- It is right in front of us. It is time we confront the real issue that holds us back from our humanity.

It's right around the corner, if we can only see the truth, if we can only see from a sentient perspective.

- I'm just fed up with no one realizing that humanity is *not inherently* screwed up. The issue that pervades keeps us in the confused, unstable state of an animal.

It's not like whackamole. That is only an animal's dumbfounded attempt to stamp out each individual surface transgression one by one rather than looking deeper into what is wrong. Look how that's worked out.

The problem is not with the individual but with humanity. Just whacking each occurrence as it crops up is a simpleton's game.

No need for laws to restrain a man that has not lost his self-respect and humanity. There may remain reasons for laws but that should be the least of them, rather than the main purpose of a legal system.

Right now, there is no thought that the human condition does *not* match human nature. "It's just the way it is." "We are only human. Ugh." Sigh.

-    Humanity need not be laid low. Most of the debacles we face are created by humanity.

Yes, natural disasters will remain (duh!). Yes, some human calamities, like car wrecks, won't go away, though road rage (and any other form of rage) should lessen considerably if not become extinct.

It's no utopia we're discussing but it is also no longer a human-induced dystopia, either.

It is an end to all of the ridiculous internecine behavior. Anything regarding human-created disasters (like war) and debacles (like abuse) can heal.

Maybe one hundred years to rid us of the worst traits from whenever we get around to starting. Human-induced disasters should all but disappear from the horizon in the not-so-distant future.

-    Maybe this is depressing me most: I spent my lifetime as a strategist. Strategy is the long game. This particular effort puts any other long game that I have experienced to shame. Meaning I will be lucky to see even the slightest start.

But, once begun, it will be like dominoes. There is only one friggin' domino that will cause all of the other delusions and offensive behaviours to finally topple.

All of my encounters, now, with the depth of surety regarding the delusions that everyone embraces, makes me think it's going to take a long time to even get in gear.

Sigh. Unless this book does a much better job of clarifying the horrible circumstances we tolerate for no good reason and the awful reason they exist.

-    It's like the lock and key to our unobstructed sentience. The animal "tradition" (instincts?) of rutting is the lock on the door behind which our sentience awaits. Men's acceptance, fulfillment, and refinement of loving a woman physically is the key that unlocks that door to a stable sentient state. That works on *so* many levels, it's downright amusing.

- Another one that has annoyed me greatly is the protestation that lasting long enough is not all it takes to make love. Duh! Of course it's not! But, it is *the crucial prerequisite* for intimate loving and everything else that has been missing from humanity and love since time immemorial. Love and our humanity have both been stunted.

- Make no mistake, it has all been downhill since we first discovered and began to make use of our sentience in a serious attempt to break free of the animal. I peg that at around the time of ancient Greece and Sophocles.

For a very short period of time, we were testing the bounds of our sentience. As we realized our failure, the attempts to free ourselves from the animal have become less and less.

- They say we use only 10% of our brain. I disagree. We use 90% of our brains to contend with the mess of delusional paradigms we have concocted that conflict with reality.

Can you imagine what it will be like when the other 90% of our brain is freed from wasting its time contending with conflicting and confusing paradigms and delusions of nonsense and absurdity?

- Nature has much more in store for a sentient being than puttering around in angst and misery. The original sin is not realizing this. The original sin is believing we are some failed experiment. That is much worse than foolishness. It is high crime and folly simultaneously.

- Emotions are *not* humanity's problem, though that often seems to be the view. *Unstable* emotions brought on by our sentience becoming confused, conflicted and distracted due to the ongoing inertia of an animal's non-sentient repertoire *is* the problem.

Emotions of a fulfilled sentient being will become stabilized by confidence and respect for oneself.

- All of our apparent chaos is due to the fact that the human race cannot be content with living the lie that has been the cornerstone of our existence.

- You think we are damaged permanently?

I *know* that we are only damaged until the human narrative can realize that we have been deceived by each previous generation that has always handed down the same folderol they were fed.

-     Incredibly, the reality of our situation is not even difficult to understand - except for the misleading paradigms embedded in each one of us that impede our enlightenment.

Our stupour, paradigms, superstitions, and delusions have done all of the talking for the last three or four millennia.

Huh.   "Formative years".   Deformative years is a better description today.

How long is it going to take us to learn that humanity is more than a failed experiment? Nature did not fail us. We have only failed ourselves - so far.

-     Some people resort to seeking something "strange" to fill the hole that is left by less than satisfactory sex. The embers are stirred by the anticipation of something new (i.e. strange), though the results never change.

Both genders desire something more but settle for something new, instead, to continue to feel that, maybe, this time they will, finally, find love and fulfillment.

Do you see the truth, yet? For a human, unfulfilling coitus leaves an emptiness.

What I suggest in order to solve the problem is so straightforward and seems to work so well. It will take effort, discipline, and forethought but we must overcome the lack.

-     We no longer need to remain an animal. An animal's witless *self*-satisfaction does not fulfill a human. That is not enough for our human heightened awareness. We care at a sentient level which we describe as love.   It includes the satisfaction of another.

There should be no confusion on this.   Heightened awareness cannot be avoided.   Part of that heightened awareness, for a man, is being aware that a woman can achieve orgasm regularly and successfully.   We care.   We are smart enough to care about fulfilling that love in its physical form. All of that potential for love turns to ashes if the physical component of love is incomplete.

\- Fulfilling coitus, unlike the facades of sexual fulfillment that are pursued by so many, does not require excess. The fulfillment of coitus is fulfilling! No desperate desire for something more remains. Just the desire to repeat the experience of physical love will remain.

Not repeat it in an obsessive manner. Obsessions are for those that are not fulfilled each time they have sex. That causes the obsessions.

\- Can you see? Loving coitus will change the landscape of humanity.

The real challenge that will remain will be mastery of our human nature. Once we shed the cloak of the animal like yesterday's clothes, that will be the challenge that remains.

In other words, just realizing there is so much more to human nature won't clear away the wreckage of more than three millennia. It only clears away the detritus remaining from the fundamental misdirection that we have taken.

Will we succeed? That is up to you.

A little off-target

\- I swear, this is like coming up for air - after fifty years of drowning in nonsense. I can breathe (most of the time). Thank goodness.

I still worry that I have not fully resolved the issue of men lasting. But, that only confirms just how important it is that we quit ignoring the reality. When I am sure that I and every man can overcome the failure, my self-respect and self-confidence is restored. Whenever I fear that there is more required, I fall apart. It is just that central to being a man.

There is something just not good about all of the fabricated twaddle of the human condition. It was like swimming through muck. A great deal of that is gone from my windshield. I hope it is gone from yours soon.

It will change your world, if you only let it. If you are at all younger than I am, you have a good chance of having a full life (I am really old).

\- It all began to clear rapidly as I realized that we sought, *always and everywhere, more than anything else*, clarity. In my instance, it was the final card that filled the hand.

Sentience is all about the desire to know what is going on. Sentience tries to correlate what is going on in order to create a mental image that reflects something consistent with the reality experienced.

When something is of crucial importance and misinterpreted (e.g. failed coitus), well, look around. It creates dystopia.

This blindspot in our sentient perspective has made it impossible to explore human nature in a robust manner. Instead, we end up with animals posing as humans and bolstering their failed self-respect in the most repugnant manners possible.

We accept all of the aberrations, from suicides to insanity to violent crimes to addiction to perversions to lunatic misinformation as if they should all exist, as if they should be expected as normal. Are you crazy??!?!

- I mention what I think of Sartre in a number of my writings. I thought I should explain why I think he irritates me so badly - besides being a leader in the intellectual dead-end of existentialism.

If I had a different ambition. If I were interested in acclaim rather than clarity and answers, I could have easily gone down the same route. I covered the same topics as that loudmouth in the past but never published them. I realized they didn't lead anywhere. All of his profound arguments are dust and ashes.

- Wow, another threat to our existence seems to be coming into focus. I was just reading that people are so disgusted, distracted, and offended by our current existence, they are no longer having children. Maybe my book is just in time. Interesting, I think, that this follows directly after my disgust in Sartre's existential despair. That wasn't on purpose, but it serves.

- It would be fascinating to do a thorough study of how each culture around the world dealt with men's failure in order to cope. While I've done a cursory examination, I think I'll leave it to others to delve deeper. It's not that important, just fascinating. Mistresses, harems, open marriages, etc.

- I just wanted to note how useful I have found the underlying principle of calculus to many endeavors. The idea of calculus is to "take it to the limit" (I also love that it is the title of an Eagles' song, as well). If you try to perceive the limits of some action or situation - the longer term effects, that is, if you take it to the limit - it can tell you a great deal, like when viewing all of the folderol of the last three thousand years and how there is no end to it if we continue to believe it is getting us anywhere. It is not.

To some extent, that is what my life has, increasingly, been about. As far as the four books go, that is completely what they are about. Maybe that is why I am so sure I am almost done. I've taken it to the limit in this book. I can do no more on my own. It is time for humanity to begin building some momentum ... or not.

There's more, of course, but there's no rush. It's not like it can't wait for humanity to get its act together. I'll leave that war to someone else.

- Instead of running around trying to make things better or stamping out each fire as it bursts into flame, *think*. It will become all the rage once we become human.

==================

Now, as you read all of this, look closely at how your paradigms have risen up to block you from rationally thinking about anything regarding sex and, especially, coitus. It short-circuits your brain as the delusions rise up.

If those walls aren't going up regularly, then I'm doing a much better job of explaining things this time around than I expect or would believe possible.

I still remember my own ramparts. Just attempt to imagine how damaging those walls have been to the human race.

- One of the strangest things about the last dozen years is the painful process I had to undertake in order to rip all of the lies out by their roots.

It was as much a necessity to force my mind to veer away from all of the nonsense every time it cropped up as it was to contemplate the real issues we have avoided so thoroughly. I can't really explain the process. I've suggested before that it is like seeing around corners or looking left while gazing right.

It was not easy to do. The nonsense is force-fed throughout a lifetime with just about anything you read or watch, not to mention being forced into place before critical thinking can develop. The nonsense is a common part of conversations and our lives. It never abates.

We are all caught up in our own paradigms of nonsense that avoid the central issue at all costs. The root cause of our misery creates an inept instantiation of sentience. It dislodges all attempts to fulfill sentience. It is utterly crazy.

- The failure of sex is like this secret that we all know and no one is willing to admit and certainly not willing to discuss. One thought that must occur to many women, at some point, has to be, "Well, that sucks." and "Men suck".

One stupid argument is that we were made that way by god. No, *animals* were made that way by creation and for good reason. Witless animals are too limited to be allowed anything but the most strict constraints in order to assure ongoing procreation. Drive it deep and get it over, no questions asked.

There is no way around it. We are more than an animal. We are different from an animal in a way that we never suspected. As long we remain only an animal, we are doomed to remain witless, demented, and very, very dangerous.

Humanity has the heightened awareness that detects the flaw in the coitus of animals. We blind ourselves to that realization, thus damaging our sentience severely.

We can't ignore what is thrown in our faces just about every day of our lives, every time we engage in sex, try as hard as we might. As long as coitus' flaw remains, we are a failed sentient race. We will remain a demented animal.

Why should we avoid making coitus into something human, as we have inadvertently done since the beginning? Since the beginning, we just carried on the fiasco. Not because we liked the idea, but because we concluded it was impossible to improve. No conscious, unrestrained, uninhibited effort was ever made to change it. I've done my best. It has, at least, convinced me we can succeed.

We also never admitted what a huge derailment the failure to improve caused.

It's not even due to the denseness of modern man. It is only due to the denseness of our early ancestors that they embedded so deeply into our consciousness as a force of inertia that we have followed right down through the ages.

One difference between then and now is that we hadn't yet created all of the divisive ways in which to regard humanity. The other is that we should know better by now.

The great thing is that our heightened intellect *can* do something about what our heightened awareness reveals.

Nature provided everything required to make coitus human, from the intelligence and insight to realize what is going on and what to do about it, to the physical characteristics (e.g. glands and such) that allow humanity to change coitus into a loving act.

I have a hard time even saying it but, at some level, there seems to be intent behind everything that Nature has done. I won't get into that further. It's certainly a freaky thought. I'll leave that for later generations to ponder. They should be better equipped. I'm just pondering the magnificence I see.

- Loving coitus needs to become as natural for a human as walking and talking. It's easier than either, though the first generation to attempt it may struggle a little. That struggle will mostly be comprised of overcoming the delusions and the fear of failure (and any abuse of their member and bad habits acquired during masturbation) that tell men to go hide their heads in the sand, thus, blunting the intellect.

Men feel helpless due to an ingrained belief that there is nothing that can be done about it, while diverting any thoughts on the subject into oblivion, often forcefully so.

That is all due to the inertia of millennia. It accounts for the ludicrous displays of manhood that are clearly nothing but a sad and pitiful cover up.

Do you think that half of the human race finally attaining a solid respect for themselves might make a difference? Are you crazy enough to think it won't??!? It sure as hell would have made a difference to me and anyone interacting with me after about my fourteenth year on this planet.

- Just think about it. Humanity dearly loves coitus. There can be little doubt about that. We certainly perform it often enough. It is crucial for the survival of the species. So, why in the world is it that unfulfilled coitus is so far down on our list of things to investigate and, more importantly, improve? The unspoken belief that there is nothing to be done speaks for itself. It is the approach of a defeated animal.

All of those web hits, for instance, on how to improve the situation confirms the belief in failure.

How can it be that we still say things like "no one has a clue why premature ejaculation happens"? More to the point, we can't even point to exactly what causes orgasm.

I have come closer to the answer than anyone. Close enough to ensure that a man and a woman can both reach climax during coitus with less effort expended than failing.

Is there more to be learned? I don't doubt it. Maybe once we get our heads out of our asses.

- I have to say it is really great to have the glamour under which we all perform like marionettes removed from my mind. It just makes me terribly sad to think that no one else has done so.

Look around. Do you really think things are working the way they are?

People are the problem. Why are people the problem, what is wrong with humanity? The answer to that is simple. We are not yet human. There is *nothing* that distinguishes us from the animal until we *really* learn to love.

- The idea that men want sex and women want love is off-base and terribly offensive. Both want and need love and sex, but love has been crushed out of each generation of the male gender. And, coitus is of little interest to women as long as it remains that of an animal in which she does not share fully in the orgasmic pleasure.

- So far, we have been stuck in the animal's take on the self-aware state, "It's all about me." That's as far as our sentient awareness has gotten.

There's only one way in which we ever take the next step and say, "It's all about being human. It's all about humanity, *not* just me."

The human race remains narcissistic.

- One of the funniest things about all of this is that no one with whom I have discussed has *ever* refuted that coitus is almost invariably one-sided and a mess. Yet, no one seems willing to admit what a huge problem that is. Crazy.

- Circumcision is another example of the distortions caused by our insanity. Worse yet, it makes overcoming the failure even more difficult (but not impossible).

Impressario

I gotta admit, I'm in awe. As we render ourselves human, we will create a work of art. Now, there's a goal. This is just the barest start on our way to humanity. There will be a lot of pioneering involved in creating a human condition that reflects human nature, the human spirit freed from delusions.

Nature is not short on miracles. Humanity is just such an example. Sooner or later, we will get there.

A couple will finally be able to make a work of art out of coitus as well as life. *That* is what it mean to be human. Humanity's natural curiosity, creativity, and imagination can finally come into play and finally be set completely free. Love as an art form.

Our current hesitant curiosity, creativity, and imagination are because we don't trust ourselves. It is like a limiter that was set on the pre-human in which we are currently ensnared.

This is liberation as it was always meant to be. We face our unlimited human potential for the first time. We liberate our humanity by learning to love.

- There is, generally speaking, a deeper layer of knowledge that goes beyond laws, science, and book learning. I just cannot determine if it is simply accessible to a sentient being that is not constantly contending with the deceit of the animal. Once we begin using that other 90% of the brain that is currently contending with the animal scams that were created in order to distract from the bumbling way we have existed for three millennia will we need the horrific level of focus I had to bring to the subject of our awareness or will a normal effort be enough for everyone?

My guess is the latter. It all has to do with that stupour. Take the dumbest seeming guy you know (that is not genetically or mentally compromised), clear out the clutter of the last three millennia that has been accepted for no good reason and you will have someone that will exceed the smartest guy you know today.

\-   So, yeah, call me furious. The intensity of thought required to drag all of these dregs of prehumanity and, especially mankind that kept scurrying around in my mind, interacting and juggling into position, was excruciating. Something close to the intensity level that I maintained for a lifetime is going to be required by all but it will be naturally occurring once the 90% of our sentient brain is recovered. It will be tempered with the revel of life, as well. Both factors will new for humanity and not onerous at all.

\-   Can you begin to see the complexity of the puzzle I had to deal with? The Nail itself is a simple thing indeed. But, all of the clutter we let infest our minds!??!?! My goodness! My goddess!

\-   I have one question for all of you. What have you learned?

Millennia

I feel like I am repeating myself occasionally. My apologies, if so. But, I am not returning to try to explain it all. This is my last book on the subject, win or lose.

I remain struck by how accurately Pandora's Box explains the situation. Most stunning for me is that the author of the myth had such incredible insight into what was really going on. It stops me cold every time I think of it. So long ago, some one saw that something was messed up regarding man and woman. It seems like they must have known exactly what was messed up.

Woman provided a gift and man made chaos out of it. That seems to pretty much sum up what has happened. Even more staggering is the insight that hope remained in the box. Incredible.

The reason men fail is because it is difficult to 1) get past all of the forced blindness, the delusions that have developed over the last few thousand years to hide the problem that the male animal does not want to admit, 2) men have fixated on the wrong questions (e.g. how to stop the end result of ejaculation rather than stopping the process in its tracks), and 3) the insight necessary to recognize the instinctual actions during rutting that cause the failure (due to brain on the fritz).

It is a tremendous puzzle that must be unobstructedly observed. The fact thay no one seems to have considered that the glands in the crotch are squeezed by certain movements while erect is beyond reason. There clearly has been some nasty delusions blocking the insight.

Is there some reason that anyone would hesitate to become good at coitus, if they believed it were possible? Do you really believe that men *like* being lousy at coitus? Any way in which the couple assures mutual satisfaction is a huge improvement. But, is it good enough?

If you are a woman, can you imagine how lousy it feels to be finished while your partner is still just getting aroused?

I don't know. Maybe the big picture is not important, but it was for me. It's where I started. One simple realization that men are generally lousy at coitus and it all came into focus *because* I was aware of the big picture.

Maybe the last, most important insight (after three books) was that the lack wasn't the biggest problem. The coverup was. The coverup, of course, wasn't intentional. It just worked out that way.

I just can't figure whether people are so caught up in their own version of lies that they cannot ever see the truth at all or is it just so overwhelming that it will take awhile to absorb the truth.

I, of course, hope it is the latter. Or, even better, would be if this book makes it clear enough for anyone to accept without delay and begin to steer humanity towards a human condition that matches our human nature. I just have a difficult time believing I have finally been clear enough or accurate enough.

We've been lying to ourselves since day one. We are deceitful because of the lie that no one has been willing to confront or admit. When that lie ends, so does the deceitful backdrop to our existence. I won't be surprised if that sounds crazy to some.

People, instead, have been trained to believe it's a terrible thing to think about sex. One never even gets to the question, why, what's wrong? So, of course, it took three thousand years to figure out that men have been caught in a trap all that time.

- We have been lying to ourselves since day one about a very specific subject. The act and art of lying was created for a reason - to hide that men are bad at coitus. All of it is so convoluted that it boggles the mind.

If I haven't stated it clearly enough, I am certain that lying is a legacy, not a constituent part of being human. It will not continue once we overcome the overwhelming lie regarding coitus that started it all.

Our thinking has become more and more dysfunctional, fractured as our condition has become more and more dystopian. We can't understand as it all seems to be going wrong. The way out is right this way.

As we continue to further accept our position as nothing more than a smart animal, our conditions have deteriorated.

The thought processes are disrupted thoroughly. It results in the acceptance of deception, the willingness to accept nonsense and absurdity as a natural way of life for a sentient being. Crazy.

In other words, existentialism and everything that goes with it. To refine the meaning of existentialism into a few words: we are born to misery. Crazy. Now I know why I despise Sarte. Existentialism celebrates our demise.

Sorry. not so. We have let ourselves be boiled in misery for no good reason. Our sentience turned up the heat.

Another that I have gone to great lengths elsewhere to explain is the constant internal assault on a man's self-respect due to the failure to bring coitus into the human realm, causing feelings of shame (never admitted, of course) and the toxic version of masculinity.

There are so many twisted thoughts that come out of the cock-up that all one needs to do is look at old men in the news. It's all there.

Lifetimes

Let's look at the "lifetime" of humanity. One can look at humanity as an infant sentient being that came into the world with no direction, guidance, to help it comprehend its substantially different existence from an animal. It is no surprise that it invented gods due to the shock at the scope of sentient awareness in order to get them through the night nor that they always chose to make their gods anthropomorphic. Maybe it was an underlying (and denied) sense of just how magnificent humanity can become.

Nor that early humanity obfuscated the sexual situation when presented with the quandary regarding coitus that fell so far beyond their wherewithal.

Love has been a tentative idea that has been around for millennia with no surety regarding its existence. Sex was hammered into shape long before humanity existed. What would lead the earliest humans to think that there was something missing? How could the link between love and coitus become substantial? It was easier to adapt the gods to provide the necessary obfuscation.

Hammerhead

We are so convinced of the status quo that there's not even a second thought. We continued rutting like animals and never looked back.

We are no longer just an animal and it is all down to loving, human coitus to make us human, sentient, loving and fulfill our human nature of sentience.

Human, sentient, loving coitus is the great liberator of our humanity.

There's gotta be someone out there with a smidgeon of intellect in their brain and a shred of honesty in their heart. Someone else that can really think and drop the act.

So far, all I see are those that would rather continue to immerse themselves in the spectacle of the animal, their endless pain, and their own compromise with sex rather than take the time necessary to let the realization dawn on them that there is so much more to humanity. Narcissism and nihilism, otherwise known as existentialism, the hopeless willingness to drown in misery is what I have seen so far. Our monstrous adaptations to the animal raises its head in argument, over and over, again.

The point is no one is culpable. We have each just found the best way to contend in the face of the ultimate lie without confronting the lie. We have all been indoctrinated into the skewed situation since birth.

It's time to get over it. We must realize that, absurdly, we remain an animal.

Close approach

I know I've mentioned this in one of the other books, but it is significant. I ran across a romance comedy movie about a writer of romance plays that makes the comment, "Well, where else is anyone going to find romance if I don't write it." How depressing. How true. It was like a slap across the face.

Do you now see that everyone of us should be enjoying a truly romantic relationship rather than reading of such in the only form it exists today: fiction? That substitute does nothing but obscure the situation.

The trees

I ran across the following statement in *Beauty & Fiction* regarding the current human condition while rereading it for the umpteenth time.   "It is so utterly witless that it leaves one breathless to contemplate."

That witlessness extends back through time to our most ancient ancestors that were certainly witless.   So, no big surprise, there.   The big surprise is how resilient the nonsense has been, how desperately we have avoided the truth.

I have conveyed our underlying problem in so many ways and, yet, I see *everyone* take the same comfort in their own personal delusions.

Young, religious heterosexual women: "I don't need no damn orgasm." Tell me that in thirty years.

Men: "Hey, I'm perfect. I am man, hear me wail." How sad.

Let's flip it on its head.   What else could finally make humanity whole? More laws, regulations, and godly decrees? Women finally training men to be loving and sentient? Better government, more money, fame for everybody?

Yeah, right.

Mutual sexual satisfaction for all in any other form? While that seems an outside possibility to me, I just have a difficult time believing it is enough. It is surely better than none, just as admitting the problem is crucial. It just doesn't seem enough to fulfill humanity's self-respect and confidence.   Today, who know?   Nothing near any of those suggestions pervades our situation.

I keep going back to that earliest time when we had the intellect equivalent to a rock.   Man, the stupid stuff they dreamed up, like all of the overblown male characteristics, now, finally, referred to as toxic masculinity! Three thousand years later!

Can't you see that highlighting toxic masculinity (or any other aberrant quality of the human condition) doesn't ever really change a thing? It is pointing our a problem without a resolution. Why does toxic masculinity exist? If you don't see the reason yet, then I have failed utterly. Without understanding why it exists, at best, it just goes underground. Sure, it may make things slightly better for women (which, of course, is a good thing) but it essentially doesn't change anything. It does not change the impetus that drives men to act inhuman. At best, it will only go underground and the genders will remain two armed camps.

The animal and the human

Men have a problem. It makes sense, really. We are based on the same general physiology of an animal. We all know it. We just remain unconvinced that humans can make something more of the act. It all comes down to application of the gifts Nature provided.

With the same physiological blueprint, it's easy to believe that nothing can be done about it. But, here is the point that we have missed for millennia. We *are* different. We *think*. Let me rephrase. We have the potential to think. When the thinking isn't obstructed by bizarre preconceived delusions, anything is possible.

Are you kidding me??!?! *Just* human??!?!? We are the most incredible artifact of an incredible universe!!! Crazily, we have avoided all of this with every fiber of our being. That, more than anything, convinces me that we can overcome anything, including lousy coitus and make it into a loving event that is so common it transforms the race.

The conditioning we endure tells us that it is evil or futile or stupid to think about making more of coitus. So, we succeed at remaining an animal. Well done.

Basically, after all of the window dressing is stripped away, that is the genesis of the phrase "grin and bear it" uttered in some sanctimonious way while our humanity remains compromised.

While avoiding the obvious insight, we have frantically tried every other trick in the book to make sex in any form work for humans. We've tried pills, surgery, appliances, frippery, perversion, cruelty, pain, and every other form of nonsense that the inventive side of humanity could dream up.

We carried on from the witless animal like nothing changed. *We* changed. Like it or not, admit it consciously or not, it won't go away.

We are sentient! We realize that there should be something more, something incredibly fulfilling about being human. We know it.

Because we fail at making coitus into a loving, human engagement, we are reduced to an animal. We continue to live through the negative aspects of a sentience that remains bestial, brought on by never attaining our humanity and fulfilling our sentient, loving nature.

We sense our humanity but it remains just out of reach. That has driven us crazy for millennia. Of late, we have been drifting further and further from our sentience and closer and closer to our animal ancestors and bestial characteristics. Big, impressive brains is all that we admit and nothing more. It has made us act more and more like rejects from the sentient pool of existence.

What is a man taught about sex? "Stick it in". That is fine for an animal. It is not what our humanity is all about.

That's the thing, you see. Animals can't learn. We can and it makes all the difference in the world. In fact, we *can't avoid* knowing that coitus should be so much more.

Like a dimwitted animal, we just *act* like we don't know it. Unlike a dimwitted animal, we can't avoid the knowledge that coitus is still an animal's endeavor. The disparity between what we know to be true and our failure to make it so causes our sentient, human, loving nature to fail utterly.

We never really took our awareness seriously. Until we do so, we remain little different from the other animals. We act like we are defined only by our intelligence, making us incredibly more dangerous, to ourselves and all other life forms, until we become human and loving.

Loving is not something you just declare (as we have attempted for three thousand years to no avail). It is not a call to arms that can be answered. It is something that is instilled in humanity and is rooted out by failing at the most significant factor of being human: the physical act of love.

There is only one way. Love has to be *internally* nurtured. It cannot be taught. It has to be fulfilled rather than beaten out of existence as we cross the threshold of puberty. Many have it mostly beaten out of them *before* puberty but that is just some of the worst animal effects extending itself from the previous generation.

Because we inadvertently avoided making coitus into something human, we could never accept the close ties that lie between love and sex. Love can only flourish for humanity once coitus is made into a human, loving, mutually pleasurable effort.

Men want sex (actually, sexual release). Big deal. That's not the problem. The problem is that they haven't figured out the best way to make it appealing to a woman and fulfilling for both. The failure cuts off the source of loving emotions in a man and leads to the woman's lack of interest in sex over time.

So, maybe a reinterpretation of the saying that men want sex and women want love is in order. Maybe a more accurate way to put it is that women, thus, understand love and men do not. There is a reason men do not. They, unlike women, cannot physically fulfill the one they love.

This may, in fact, be the primary source of confusion. Women just don't get what is wrong with men. Again, it is a matter of inertia. Men have always been off-kilter and women have alway had to put up with it.

The bigger problem is that our sentient awareness becomes more refined. We understand more and more as humanity progresses through existence. More and more, we see the problems and despair because we see no resolution. That is what I am attempting to change.

A man may overcome the worst of the side-effects and act human. He may even mimic being human rather well. That is quite an accomplishment. Almost alway due to the loving effects of a woman. That does not make him human. It makes him a wretched creature attempting to sidestep the insanity (but, never the misery) of the inhuman condition. Kudos for those that make the effort, but it's not enough.

Over and over again, the momentum moves toward frustration, the finer qualities are abandoned, and the human race goes into upheaval, once again. We are approaching that point, once again.

While the man's urge for sex lasts most of a lifetime, the woman's urge wanes as she realizes she is getting the short end of the straw. She does not have the relentless drive for sex. That disparity, of course, exacerbates the problems.

Once we realize that making coitus into something human is what makes us human, the next stage of evolution of humanity can begin. Lovingkindness can become more than a word in a dictionary.

Coitus is more than just an urge, an itch that a man must scratch. It encompasses our lives. It makes us alive in more ways than one.

It can also make us human.

Men's urge for sex is physically driven. That alone is enough to drive a guy frantic but it certainly is not enough to derail his humanity.

Failure to make coitus into something human is. Even with all of a man's best intentions in the world, it cannot fail to damage a man's sentient nature to know that he has failed at the most human act.

The disparity builds up over a lifetime to drive him crazy and drive him away from all of the qualities that distinguish a human from an animal. It is not the urge to sex that causes the problem. *It is the inability to make sex into something human that causes the problem.*

Now, imagine a world in which all the couples in the world are having great coitus and really enjoying it. How crazy is that idea? Today, it mostly only exists in the pages of fiction, romance novels and porn.

This is not porn. It is your life we're talking about.

Does anything else explain why so many people swear up and down that sex is a curse laid on mankind? To listen to some groups, you would think that humanity would be better off without sex - or a brain (i.e. return to the animal domain). Just think about that statement for a minute. Crazy doesn't even begin to describe it. The contrived duplicity of those suggestions are remarkable.

We have duped ourselves so throughly that we can't see that bringing coitus to a sentient level is what makes us human. Instead, we focus only on our intellect alone. Look where that has gotten us. People seem unable to distinguish a lie from the truth. Political correctness has become all the rage for some. Lying through your teeth, admitting nothing, always suggest that you did nothing wrong is another reaction that appears when someone is caught (especially high profile idiots). Do you see where it is all leading? Maybe not.

Love, the essence of sentience and our humanity, in all of its varied forms and tremendous magnificence cannot be fulfilled without making coitus into something human.

Do you see the joke on mankind? Male animal wants sex. Male animal gains sentience and becomes human, at least in form. Man finally begins to scratch his head, thinking to himself, "you know I think the woman could enjoy this as much as me and, and, and ... oooohhhhhh, that was wonderful! What was I saying?"

Only humanity can succeed at loving, in the physical as well as the emotional sense. Is it a surprise that men's emotions are all over the map as they continue to fail at the physical component?

So far, we have only excoriated ourselves and cursed our very existence. The truth is that there is something wrong about coitus, something incomplete in the animal instantiation of coitus for a sentient being.

We became aware that animal coitus is not fulfilling. Animal coitus just gets the job of impregnation done. Until it becomes the common case that there is *mutual* satisfaction, it will remain out of balance with sentience.

We know better. We just have to realize that we can do something about it and quit playing the role of a fool.

But, here's the last laugh, the real twist, the joke of all jokes, and the misery of the last few thousand years. If men had not been so embarrassed by the problem as to never assemble their industrious and inventive wits as a gender to face the problem, men would have discovered long ago that it's...just...dead...easy to love.

Even though it is easy, it does take some explaining in our current utterly befuddled state. As it becomes common knowledge, it will also become a natural extension of being human, like talking or walking on two legs. Call it a second generation instinct *not* to plunge immediately as deep as possible. Geez, we might even talk about it and improve it further. It takes some slight effort but nothing a human can't handle easily. The effort is mostly just throwing off the animal instincts that have driven sex for millions of years.

If you have some idiotic notion that it is bad to do things that are not 'natural', then what are you doing talking, reading, writing, or walking on two legs? Forget driving a car, riding a bike, or listening to music. Go back to your cave and scratch your ass.

All of the inconsistencies of which we all take part are due to the inability to see what is right in front of us: coitus must be something more, something uniquely human.

Roots

Excuse my ongoing agitation. I am just so afraid that I am still not explaining it all well enough. I also realize that some of my thoughts remain tentative. I am not tentative, though, about the root cause of our problems.

I hope like hell I am wrong and some are slowly getting it. Excuse my impatience and excuse me if I seem to be going to extraordinary lengths to try to explain. This will be my last effort. So, I'm trying to put everything I can into the effort, including the kitchen sink.

I realize how difficult it is to absorb this, due to the conflagration of nonsense that has assaulted our consciousness since the beginning. That doesn't make it any easier for me to tolerate the failure of others to accept the truth when it is laid out before them. I had to do it all on my own without any help or outside insights. So, no, I'm not complacent. I am annoyed as hell.

Worse yet, I am still uncomfortable as to whether I have resolved the issue well enough for men. I hope I have but I always admit to myself. I have no doubt that, if humanity puts the blinders away and begins a concerted effort, it can be overcome to an extent far exceeding my measly efforts. I feel very good about the insights regarding the glands. Even if I have not completely resolved the issue, I feel confident that humanity can.

Let's try looking at it a different way.

A man gains an uncomfortable feeling that something is wrong. At some level of consciousness, he knows he's not as good at coitus as he knows he should be. Worse yet, he may wonder if he is only one of few. All of the fiction that portrays so much success would sure lead him to think that the problem is isolated. His whole orientation towards both genders is affected in many ways. Let's examine the usual adaptations.

The man begins looking for someone that will tolerate his pitiful excuse for coitus since he really wants to get laid. That supplants the desire to express his love or to look for love. He'll say the words if it helps get a woman in bed.

In the face of their ever-present failure, men consider all other men competitors. He is seldom sure that anyone does as poorly as he does.

His lack of confidence in himself turns into lack of self-respect for himself. It becomes much, much more important for him to get laid rather than have a loving relationship.

He needs to find someone that will tolerate him and his pitiful attempts at coitus. Remember, this is all his perception, no matter what the woman feels about it. He puts on airs to cover up his feelings of inadequacy. He becomes a facade.

From a woman's point of view, coitus is not a big deal. At least, not early in life. So what if the sex is not spectacular. Who cares? It makes her man happy - or less irritable.

As life progresses without coitus becoming something desirable, she realizes the tremendous satisfaction that the man attains. Why should she be only the vessel for his sexual satisfaction, over and over and over and over, again? At best, the anticipation of something good finally gets supplanted by the realization that it is *only* arousal and anticipation of satisfaction and seldom the actual event.

Let's say the man finds some woman that is more than willing to accept the incompetent coitus or some substitute - for the short term. Just like the man's initial adaptation, there are an infinite number of branches that the next adaptation may take. Initially, he will be relieved.

He may be suspicious of why the woman is willing to accept such lousy sex. It will probably never cross his mind that it is because womanhood is used to sex being less than satisfactory, nothing more than a crapshoot in which she always loses. It is "acceptable" - at least until they decide "acceptable" is not good enough. A near certainty is that, at some point, the woman is going to become less interested and willing to engage in unsatisfactory coitus.

As this happens and his own self-respect continues to erode, he will put on further airs to convince himself that he is a man, thus toxic masculinity is born. If he finds another woman that is attracted to him (usually, a younger woman that is much less experienced with men's failure), he may very well want to do something about it in order to prop up his ego with the desperate and bizarre hope that something has changed. He has no idea what. He just wants that sense of love to fulfill, which it never does.

Well, anyways, I don't want to go further into it. I went through a number of scenarios in *Sentience* to describe some of the various situations. I just thought this introduction to the mindsets leading to the various fiascoes was worthwhile.

One of the oddest facts regarding all of this is that many women truly believe (at least early in life) that orgasm is just not that important to them. That also is part of the problem. In many ways, it is just as dimwitted as the man's perspective.

It also denies our humanity. Just like with men, women realize the real story as they age. The biggest difference being that women lose interest in coitus. For some time now, that has not necessarily meant they lose interest in orgasm.

Another perspective

Let's shift our focus to the human condition. We accept so many lies. It becomes almost second nature for many. We become inured to all of the deceit. We don't even see half of the lies as they pass under our noses.

It is because we don't recognize the most essential lie. We have avoided the big lie for so long that we lose our sense for truth.

We also don't seem to notice the daily casual acts of inhumanity or the calamity of our current conditions. After all, "we are *only* human". We shrug it off because "that's just the way it is", no matter what we have heard about love.

The internal compass of morals and respectable behaviour that should guide us, *without external inducements* (e.g. laws, peer pressure, etc), is absent *because our humanity* has never developed.

Now that I've stripped away the facade, ripped away the curtain, I can see all of the casual offensiveness that we endure. It's truly horrible.

Do you really think that's our nature? Nature is about improvement. For the frothing animal that we remain, 'improvement' is through fear, dominance, and blunt force. That's no improvement at all for a sentient being.

We have followed the course laid out by the dumb animals that preceded us. Cower in fear. *Act* like a human, whatever that means.

Nature attempted something very different with us. It gave us a potential that we have barely imagined, much less fulfilled.

Lying is the act of a demented animal. You can bet that self-respect goes down before anyone indulges in lying freely and without remorse.

We have the ability to seriously manipulate our existence and our environment either for improvement or destruction. We have excelled at destruction. We build a little and, then, we tear it all down.

When will we accept that the phrase "we're only human" is the most offensive, debilitating phrase ever uttered?

Another take

People look around and seem to say to themselves, "we're okay". I'm just not sure what they think is okay. Is it just themselves and their immediate friends? Do they blind themselves to all of the pain and suffering of humanity (if they are not immersed in it)? Do they blind themselves to all of the offenses that humanity mounts against humanity? Do they voice their mantra of peace, hoping it will all go away or, at least, not bother them?

Almost everyone likes to believe in some religion, some saviour for humanity, as long as that saviour is not humanity itself. They also shed those religious beliefs in a heartbeat anytime someone crosses them or whenever it seems inconvenient to rely on some nebulous god.

Then, the animal really shows itself. Our spirituality, morals, and ethics are flimsy because it doesn't come from within the individual. It all remains an act. It is an instruction manual regarding how to *act* human in the face of forces that corrupt our humanity. It is putting on airs.

Underneath all of the excuses, we are utterly convinced we are no more than the animals that came before us - just far more dangerous.

When will we rely on humanity to save itself? The gods are nothing but crutches for an animal that has not attained its humanity. When will we quit throwing up our hands as if our fate were not in our own hands?

What will it take for humanity to rely on itself? You should know the answer by now.

And another

Can you think of any good reason for men to be pleased with lasting two minutes? Do you really think they pat themselves on the back? Does it soften the blow of failure if you only last three minutes?

Is it just a way to allow acceptance of their failure? All the men gather round and tell themselves, "Well, at least I'm doing as well as can be expected". Underneath that facade, though, the human is crying out.

Can you think of any good reason that men cannot learn to last long enough to love a woman thoroughly during coitus? Can you think of any good reason men should not learn to indefinitely delay ejaculation? Can you think of any good reason that a man should not be able to love a woman thoroughly?

Oh, by the way, if any man out there has completely resolved the issue of indefinitely delayed ejaculation and knows exactly what they are doing that is different, please, please, please don't be shy. Don't think it is anything other than a huge deal *for all of humanity.* Don't even think it is a way to be better than the rest of the men. Please, shout it out.

The whole fiasco reminds me way too much of a caveman cowering in his cave, afraid to come out and face the world. Instead, he gets together with his caveman cohorts and declares that two minutes is good enough. Theres' a plan.

Can you think of any good reason that men have proclaimed two minutes good enough? Especially, considering women need more like ten minutes? Does it make men feel good to think that it has been officially declared that lasting two minutes is good enough?

Or, is it just that men think it is too difficult or impossible to achieve indefinitely delayed ejaculation, hence the coverup?

Are they so immersed in their misery that they never even give it a thought? Are they taught it would be evil to learn how to last long enough to satisfy a woman? Or, is it that they just don't think at all? Millennia of conditioning and my own past experience make me think they are taught to not dare to look too deeply.

Man or woman

If your unassisted coitus with someone of the opposite sex has been completely fulfilling, then it is likely you will not be able to accept what I am saying. That seems highly unlikely to be the case for the vast majority of humanity.

If it is not, if your heterosexual experience has been less than the dream, rather than believe all of the fiction that is thrown at you, please consider what I say. I am certain that the deeper you look, the more certain you will become.

Forget the fiction and look at *your own* experience. Mine, at least, I can now admit was an utter disaster.

I really doubt that there is a significant number of those that will honestly say their experience with coitus has been completely fulfilling. It won't be completely fulfilling until the man waits upon the woman's fulfillment without the slightest concern.

Tacking with the wind

From a completely different perspective, can you entertain the thought that it need not be a long, drawn out process in order for humanity to attain its sentience? Can you imagine that, so far, we have just taken the wrong tack?

We are a highly sensitized, intelligent race. We should be able to achieve a human existence in short order (by that, I mean replacing, "we are only human" with "Omigoodness! We are HUMAN!!!!")?

Can you believe that just maybe we get there by a different means than browbeating the beast into the shape of a human?

Can you think of a factor, other than loving coitus, that seems so fundamental to loving and so thoroughly out of skew? Can you think of another aspect of life that we avoid discussing (but never performing) at all costs?

Can you understand that it is not a matter of this or that individual attaining a sentient state? It has to become part of human consciousness, the human narrative.

Forget good and bad. The terms are nonsense. There is sentient and non-sentient.

A few individuals achieving loving sex does not cut it. Sure, those individuals would lead a better life but it is not enough to transform the race. The forces of non-sentience will still remain.

As long as we refuse our sentient perspective, we will remain a mess. We will remain lost.

Avoidance

The other issues that each individual faces can be extrapolated. I shouldn't need to get into them. Each individual should be able to do the extrapolation themselves.

Maybe my underlying fury is because I spent a lifetime ridding myself of all of the bullshit in which humanity bathes itself with no help from anyone and, then, I run into so many that won't even make the attempt with a lot of the groundwork already laid out for them?

I suffered through a lifetime because I would not settle, I would not accept or justify bullshit. Surprising to me, even with everything I have detailed, people cannot see past their own delusions and make the jump.

When I first started exploring this radical departure from the animal's viewpoint, there was one particularly that stuck in my head. A man online proclaimed that "God did not make sex for women to enjoy."

Talk about the ultimate self-serving use of a god! That statement, more than most, shows the self-serving way in which religious beliefs substituting for spiritual certainty have been twisted (by animals impersonating a human) in order to support our delusional, superstitious, deceitful way and justify failure and destruction.

My own desperate desire for something other than the nonsense, absurdity, and misery that we endure seems shared by few, if any.

Once again, I have to desperately ask that you contemplate your own situation in juxtaposition to all of the fiction that is fed to you. All of those quips and sexual innuendoes implied by the tv shows, books, and movies, as well as the conversations you have had with others, should be questioned in context of your own sexual situation. Any nonsense, especially your own, needs to be ruthlessly rooted out in order to get at the truth of the situation.

Accepting the status quo or the politically correct answers will not get you there.

The true situation is that we have been so heavily brainwashed, generation by generation, that there is nothing you can confidently believe other than your own experience.

Initially, it will be a wrenching change but it is necessary.

The animal fiasco

Do you think there is a single man alive that *likes* being bad at coitus? Do you think a man would pass up the chance to be good at coitus, the most incredible feeling of fulfillment, if he thought it was possible in a most natural manner?

Sometimes, I believe women are just so used to men being so bad at coitus that they think it's just laziness on the men's part. ***He doesn't even know that it's possible to do better!*** So, he hides in his confusion in shame, thus confusing the situation further.

There is no evidence that men can be good at coitus. If you search the web, you will find innumerable suggestions. None of which really work. Most of them won't even extend the experience to a few minutes.

Still, I assure you, it is completely possible for a sentient, thinking race to make something more from the dregs of coitus that animals endure. Extending the experience, to the delight and fulfillment of *both* participants, can take place in a natural manner that feels utterly human. It can make something more of the experience and the human.

It should become utterly easy as we gain confidence and surety.

The past failures to find resolution are all because of the conditioning in delusions and paradigms of nonsense which led to the question never being asked properly.

More evidence

We gave up on making coitus a human experience long ago. The evidence is everywhere. The failure is so deeply ingrained in the human condition that it is just accepted. It is so deeply embedded in our brains that we scramble to avoid facing the truth. In its fulfillment lies our humanity.

The subject of sex

The suppression of the subject of sex is one of the most long-standing and obvious examples of evidence of the unfulfilled promise of mutual sexual pleasure and the disastrous results of not achieving it.

Men pretty much rule our existence and love having sex and, yet, the discussion of sex is suppressed. Pretty strange. Men also seldom talk about sexually satisfying a woman. Though many will talk endlessly about their sexual exploits, "conquering" a woman.

This has derailed every consideration of sex in a coherent, rational manner. Instead of addressing the problem head on, we have prevaricated in the most bizarre manner.

Because we still can't face the truth, we have been avoiding direct confrontation with the dilemma of failed coitus. We will talk and experiment with just about anything else regarding sex, including any perversion of the highest order that the human mind can create, but we will damn well not discuss how lousy coitus tends to be.

Men

All of men's current primary characteristics can be traced back to men's quandary regarding coitus. The bluster, the desperate desire to seem manly, the toxic caricature of masculinity, the whining all indicate that something is seriously wrong. The link to coitus is unarguable.

Stupour

While I argue against the stupid direction of all of our current efforts to change things (which never change anything at all regarding humanity itself), do not mistake that for a belief that humanity is stupid. We are not.

We are in a stupour caused by the difficulty of facing the realization that human coitus should be radically different from animal coitus. Rutting is not making love and it drags us back to the animal state every time we perform it. It becomes so conditioned into us that we pass it on to the next generation as we finally accept "that's just the way it is."

"Evidence"

It offends me that I should need to explain this but I'm not doing another book, so I don't dare leave this out. I don't think it will do any good for anyone wailing for evidence but I must try. Something's not getting through and that blows me away. I'm throwing the kitchen sink at it this time.

I continue to be amazed that anyone asks me for "evidence". What do you think these four books were all about? Look in the mirror. You are avoiding the evidence.

Does it take evidence to convince you that our earliest ancestors were dumber than a bag of hammers? More animal than human? Does it take some great leap of insight to realize that they didn't know what to think regarding the very human dilemma of coitus?

The proof, the evidence, of that is right in front of your nose. Only if you have had nothing but mutually satisfying coitus can you refute it.

Do you need evidence that coitus is not working right for a sentient race? Does the proclamation that men that last two minutes are doing well while women need more like ten minutes to achieve orgasm mean nothing to you? Does that not compute?

Are you really satisfied with something less? Does any other way in which to provide mutual satisfaction fulfill you? Do you never wonder what it would be like to share that fulfillment while gazing into the eyes of your lover? Would you avoid it if you knew it was possible?

Or, do you believe that it is better to ignore what our sentient awareness has always told us: that there is more to coitus than an animal ever imagined? Do you need evidence to convince you that women like orgasms, also? Don't you think it odd that we have found other ways to seek mutual sexual satisfaction but have never done anything regarding the most natural, loving physical act of sex? Do you think using a pill, the tongue, or a dildo can substitute for the most natural act of engaging in coitus? It is surrender. We surrender more each day.

Or, maybe you need more evidence that men can last indefinitely. I do, also. I've provided evidence regarding why men fail to last, an explanation of why ejaculation occurs and how to prevent it. Nothing will substitute for all men *knowing* they are good at coitus.

What will it take to prove to you that there is something wrong with a race that hides from the fact that men can't provide the most glorious delight possible in life to his woman through the most natural method that nature provided?

Do you point to fictional depictions of coitus for proof that coitus is okay? Do you discount your own experience?

How in the world does anyone need proof that something is wrong between the two sexes? It is so much like two armed camps as to take one's breath away. Do you need evidence regarding the abuse men heap down on anyone they can, especially women? How about the daily news?

Can you possibly be so dense as to still want to focus on the isolated events, the individual crimes rather than the big picture?

No, what really stunts a man's humanity is knowing that he's hiding from his failure, hiding from the feeling that he is helpless in the face of his failure, often foolishly believing it is just him. Do you not see this all shows itself blatantly in the conduct of so many men?

The only thing for which I cannot provide proof is that love is initiated in the physical domain and that we really haven't a clue, yet, when it comes to love. I think the proof of three thousand years of the failure of *thinking* ourselves into a loving mindset would be enough for you to, at least, consider the proposal. Animals can't love. Humans can.

The evidence that we have become utterly confused on the topics of sex and love is everywhere.

The proof that the subject of sex is taboo is everywhere.

If I sound acerbic, you've got that right.

The evidence is available and documented regarding the offensive behaviour of men towards women, though I don't think it is needed, that one in three women are abused, which I am certain is an underestimate if you define abuse as violence in any form, including verbal, mental, and betrayal. And, the latest, what is now called micro-aggressions, is just further proof that training men only makes the offenses go underground.

Maybe the link between the failure of animal sex to satisfy our heightened awareness and the offensive nature of men towards women is just too much for you. It doesn't really matter, one in three women being abused at some point in their lives is enough to prove *something* is seriously wrong.

If you have a better suggestion for why this occurs, I am more than willing to listen. Just, don't wave your arms around and say, "men are bad." or "It's just some men." or "It's not only men."

Two armed camps and no one is winning.

We pout our lives away. Should I go through all of the common phrases, once again? "We are only human" is just the top of my list. "That's just the way it is" is right up there. Existentialist despair is another.

Do you need evidence to realize that we can do better at coitus? Do you need evidence to prove that a man would like to satisfy his woman sexually while inside of her?

Does it take evidence to convince you that we are not doing very well as a sentient race? Do you need evidence to be convinced that there should be something more than existentialism? That all of our attempts to become better humans in the past have been all for naught?

Do you need evidence that we have been going downhill for quite a few centuries as we thrash around? That we are getting no closer to an emotionally balanced, rational existence and much closer to destroying ourselves?

Do you really believe our human condition is the best we can do? Do you really think laws, and pounding the pulpit is what it takes to become a loving and human race? Do you really believe we are getting any closer to something sentient, loving?

How do I prove that humans are broken because the human race has not raised coitus to a human standard or, at least, identified the dilemma in order to address it seriously?

The "evidence" is in the fact that there is something wrong with a sexually sentient race that cannot admit that there is more necessary for a sentient version of coitus. It is there in the fact that the mention of sex is taboo. It is there in the fact that men, after three thousand years can do no better than rut. Don't you dare shrug your shoulders.

The strongest evidence of all is that we don't even admit that there is a problem with coitus. That we create fictions that represent fulfilling coitus but never the reality.

We point it out in so many indirect ways but we are never willing to state it outright. The jokes in the sitcoms about the man lasting just long enough to get his rocks off and, then, going directly to sleep.

Any romantic comedy assures you that the woman is satisfied during coitus. The evidence is that it occurs in fiction regularly but not so much in real life (e.g. two minutes versus ten). If it isn't stated outright in the romcom, it is implied. Only if your own experience with unassisted coitus has been fully satisfactory can you possibly argue. I don't expect to hear any argument on that basis.

It wasn't stupidity that caused us to avoid realizing that something is missing. It was stupour. That is the only possible reason for it to have taken humanity three thousand years to figure it out. The stupour and deceit need to end. That is the heart and soul of our disruption.

Mince the words as you please, we have been deluded and the delusions and deceits have extended themselves into every corner of our existence. If you cannot admit that you have bought into a fiction, no amount of "evidence" is going to change your mind.

If you are repulsed by the idea of every man being able to satisfy their lover during coitus, that is evidence of its own. Why else would anyone argue so hard against the idea?

Aaaarrrrgggghhhhhh!!!!!!!!!!!!!!!!!!!

The completed sentient state is a heightened state of *unobstructed* awareness. Of course, every living being has some level of awareness.

We exceed the level of awareness of any other life-form on Earth by a long shot. Where we fall short is that our awareness is anything but unobstructed. A huge factor in that obstructive veil is the lack of loving coitus. It may be the only obstructive veil.

Whether coitus alone accounts for all of the nonsense, misery, and horror that we tolerate, we will just have to see, *if we ever get over our delusions and look at sex and coitus without compromise, without delusion and resolve our issues*.

Evolution

What we don't seem to be able to comprehend is that evolution is different for humans. It is not just genetics that makes humans something more than an animal. Nature in the form of genetics gave us the potential, the tools, that can conclude in something human, something special.

Unabated, undistorted awareness and its application is key to achieving the evolutionary hurdle of fulfilling our sentience, our human nature, and the finer qualities that have so eluded us. Clarity is key.

The rest, the knowledge, intellect, curiosity, creativeness all follow the lead of the heightened awareness. If that awareness is obstructed, the rest are compromised. The "knowledge" is tainted, the curiosity and intellect are blunted, the creativeness is distorted.

It is up to us to clear away the last debris from our animal heritage to arrive at something human. For humanity, it is more than just accepting the witless change in our genes. Consciousness must align with our awareness by no longer tolerating delusions.

It is all about clarity.

It is crucial that humanity honestly assesses its ongoing situation with its awareness undiminished by the nonsense and absurdity that we have accepted for so long without question.

I look at all of the ways in which humanity lies to itself, concocts utterly ridiculous justifications for its heinous actions and shake my head. What is wrong with us? What is wrong with humanity? We are not yet human and sentient.

Humanity must come to terms with its awareness rather than subjugate it. Untarnished awareness is the missing element in human evolution. Clarity must prevail.

Sex is our blindspot. We have been completely bogged down in misinformation since the beginning due to that.

The Castalian spring

We just delay putting away all of the misery and deceit that we have built into an absurd structure by declaring it all senseless. The way we fight to retain this state of fatuous, daft existence appalls.

I can only lead the jackass to water. It's up to them to drink deeply of the Castalian Spring.

Paradigm logic

There is no logic to our paradigms and that is the point. Our current paradigms are so constructed as to bypass any attempt at logic, short-circuit the human ability to think, avoid looking at what is really going on because we fear it. Clarity has become obscurity.

The worst paradigms create conclusions that are completely absurd and have nothing to do with logic and, thereby, break humanity's ability to think. They are a knee-jerk reaction that we tell ourselves. We accept them and do nothing other than comply. We let them rule us.

Centerpiece

I have tried and tried to make it clear that it is not *about* men lasting as long as necessary. That is only the precursor, the starting point from which humanity can become human. I honestly believe that no other form of mutual satisfaction can compare to loving coitus. Men lasting long enough is only that which must come before men can learn to ***make*** *love* and, thereby, become human and loving.

We must open the floodgate that will finally let the loving, sentient perspective flow in men and finally unleash the loving sentient perspective that has always been present in women.

The failure of men to provide sexual satisfaction causes the failure of the loving engagement that is quintessentially human. The failure disables the ability of men to think past the failure and humanity to even perceive what making love (the act) is really all about.

Coitus is not ever going away. It will continue. Is there any reason for it to remain enacted like a rutting animal? Is there any reason that humanity should go on seeking other ways to provide mutual sexual satisfaction, other than coitus? Somehow, that seems to be the conclusion, so far. It is a far cry from a fulfilled sentient state.

A human sentient perspective is stunted in any man that cannot succeed at sharing the physical fulfillment eye to eye. His emotions remain stunted and all over the map, thus he remains stunted as a human being that more resembles an animal.

Indefinitely delayed ejaculation is not the sum total of what sex is about. It is only the necessary precursor for the human engagement that frees a man's awareness from the horrors of feeling like a failure and the horrors of remaining just an animal. It is all about releasing the sentient perspective of love in a man and, thus, his humanity.

Selflessness

Right now, humanity is so deranged that the only word to describe it is parasitic. Humanity is parasitic towards itself and everything else in existence. We mindlessly bleed everything around us, including other humans in our attempts to exist. As we seek our humanity and fail, we distort everything regarding our existence. That distorts everything we touch. Hence, parasitic.

Mutually beneficial behaviour can be proven (and has been by game theory) to *always* be the best solution. A win-win situation is always better. Duh.

Sound familiar? Or does the lose-lose situation of heterosexual relationships sound familiar?

Our existing approach to intimate relationships is anything but mutually beneficial and its effects are reflected in all of society, culture, and the workings of humanity. Humanity's existence, undifferentiated from an animal, begins with coitus that is *not* mutually beneficial, *not* human. We have continued to fracture in its absence. We have been given the genetic gifts that must be accompanied by clarity in order to become human. The physical limitations are a mirage.

Men have always attempted to coerce women into sex (e.g. the club over the head, evolving into paying for it in one way or another). Why would that be so if it were a mutually beneficial relationship?

That coercion reflects all of the more sinister behaviours of men towards women (e.g. misogyny, abuse, sex trade, rape, sexism, micro-aggressions, pedophilia &c).

Mutually beneficial intimate relationships changes everything. It fulfills our humanity.

We are also hard-wired to tell the truth. Telling a lie is extremely difficult and, yet, we currently excel at it. Do I need "evidence" for that, as well??!? Headlines, diplomacy.

Human expression

We have warped every expression of our humanity into something disfigured, vile. Even love. The lust that we accept as a substitute for love is not human.

"Falling in love" is not love. It is the desperate desire to rely on someone else to validate one's existence. It is some parody of human loving. It is the absence of self-respect and confidence that makes us wish to rely on someone else for validation.

I'm guessing these attempts to make you think are a waste of my time but I feel I have to give it one last try.

Fiction

All around, you will see loving couples that are sexually satisfied and live lives happily ever after - in fictional accounts.

(Except for the book version of *A Princess Bride* by Morgenstern. It is truly brilliant. That may be the only honest fictional romance ever written - it goes on beyond the "happily ever after". It is incredibly refreshing to read).

Coital satisfaction exists in fiction because we know it *should* exist and, in relatively rare instances, maybe it does, though that is still uncertain. If it does, someone should have passed along their insights for coital success long ago.

We know that there should be something more and we remain devastated. We seek madly about for some other form of sex as a substitute, thus distorting all in its path, while the correct answer has been right in front of us the whole time. Obsessions, aberrations, and perversions are the result. It is almost like the suppressed coital situation makes us all run for cover.

The best situation, under the current strictures, seems to be to find some way to come up with ... I got nothin'. I try to come up with some alternative way for a sentient race to fulfill and maintain a fully rational, emotionally balanced, and undeceived state without satisfying the essential sentient physical need coupled with the emotional need that leave the sentient awareness unobscured and I've got nothing. Anything else is a stopgap. All of the surface issues and all of the ways we attempt to circumvent lousy coitus are stopgap measures that just exacerbate the damage.

Admitting the issue and providing clarity would be a big step in the right direction, but without fulfilling the potential for love between man and woman, we fail.

If it weren't possible for men then, sure, we would have to try to find something else but the results are uncertain. Without loving coitus, I think we are at a standstill.

Still, it is certainly better to know what is going on. Clarity is essential to our awareness. I am beginning to despise the phrase "perception is reality" almost as much as "we're only human."

Contemplate your navel? Doesn't really work as it is only improving *your* existence while the rest of humanity continues to crumble around you. That is not a solution. That is just another narcissistic, nihilistic dodge.

Any other form of mutual satisfaction improves the situation but doesn't seem to resolve it. I could be wrong on that. If every man found some way in which to satisfy their lover, it would be a huge improvement and maybe enough. I just don't think it will fulfill our human nature.

No excuses

This is not an excuse for men's ongoing lousy behaviour. Many men rise above the disturbance to their situation. So, this is not an excuse for being an offensive asshole.

Still, avoiding being an asshole is not the same as becoming lovingly human. The concept of a man that *acts* loving is nothing other than an act without ever fulfilling the obligation necessary to transcend the state of the animal. A vague sense of love is better than the other current alternatives but still just leaves them as an example of roadkill on the route to human life.

This that I am attempting to lay out describes that something is wrong with our whole existence. The fog of obscurity continues to distort our sentient awareness, our clarity regarding existence. Clarity is essential.

This is not toxic male arrogance trying to find an excuse for the current horrible behaviour of many men. This is rational, miserable, fierce human certitude that the only resolution to that which upsets the human tapestry is loving expressed in its physical form. Its natural fulfillment is through loving coitus. It is impossible for a man to fulfill that loving impetus until he can physically love, fulfill his mate as well as himself, not just rut.

He must learn to give as well as take. It is up to men to make the change.

All of humanity must realize what it takes in order for coitus to become human. Whether every man needs to achieve that potential is not even a rational question. Once men are certain it is possible, they will line up in droves. Men becoming loving will not be an issue once it is clear that men can perform coitus as men have always dreamed. This is the one situation in which he needs control of his own actions. Discipline, forethought, and knowledge are all that are required.

Everyone achieving a loving, intimate relationship with another is a completely different issue. It is *not* crucial. The confidence instilled by knowing one will *not* fail when presented with the situation is crucial to retaining one's self-respect. That the result is certain and that those of humanity that are blessed enough to attempt it consistently achieve it will transform the human race.

Split Personality

The current human condition is much like a split personality. It is split between the ongoing animal ravages and the desire to achieve something human, something sentient. The desire to achieve something human is invariably crushed under the boot of the animal ravages as long as the animal remains.

I started out the book mentioning two schools of thought on what it means to be human. Those can be viewed as the two primary branches of the split personality of humanity. That is just the beginning. From there, it splits and splits and splits into utterly nonsensical divisions.

Maybe the best explanation of that split personality is the earlier description of the quandary of free speech. There are just *no* good answers until we become human.

In the meantime, we split along lines into at least two camps regarding nearly everything. Humanity is full of these divisions. Everyone grasps for something that makes the most sense to them in a situation that makes no sense at all. It is all down to not yet becoming human and gaining a sentient perspective.

I could list so many examples from governments to religions to political parties to who ends up being the saviour for the exact same god. "Mine is better than yours. Nya, nya, nya. Mine's the *real* one!" But what would be the point until we become human? The nonsense of all 'sides' will become glaringly apparent in the light of a human, loving perspective, our illustrious human nature. I do not pretend to fully understand what that perspective will be, other than human and far different from the animal.

The split personality becomes more pronounced as humanity continues to move through life. The truth gets further shattered. Along with all of the distortions and untruths of our condition, we pick up tiny pieces of the truth that fit in with one of the many distorted views of a sentient existence that suits our nihilistic, narcissistic desires. We accept partial truths. The spilt usually runs along the lines of whether we are an animal or something more that we have not yet attained.

It is split right down the middle, the majority belief swaying between the belief we are no more than a smart animal to a surety there is something more. Mostly depending on the degree of calamity humanity is currently enduring. When it gets bad enough that we are destroying large portions of our existence, humanity, once again, attempts to right itself from the lunatic animal desires that always wreak so much havoc when predominant.

The choices are diametrically opposed. As the human condition goes to hell in a hand-basket, the animal prevails. All because some adopt in full the nihilistic, narcissistic perspective. As we attempt to pick up the pieces, once again, fewer remnants of our humanity prevail each time.

Each split picks up pieces of the truth that suits their experience and mentality. I've often wondered whether anyone acknowledges to themselves how incomplete their view is. For each split, there are huge holes and inconsistencies. Does anyone ever admit the gaping holes in the views they adopt? Do they shrug it off as the best fit for circumstances? Do they justify, rationalize in some bizarre manner? Is "pick a side" the most important consideration? For a witless animal.

Choices of extremes

There are no good answers to the human condition as long as we remain nothing more than demented animals. Humanity creates all of the disturbing issues with which humanity has to contend. *We are the problem*, until we become human.

The realist and the dreamer represent the split personality well.

The realist accepts things as they are and is often willing to wreak havoc to get what they want. After all, being practical, one concludes that we are just animals. Take what you want, force your view to be accepted, and to hell with humanity. Lie, cheat, and steal to your heart's content. The golden rule becomes, "don't get caught."

The dreamer looks for something more and is willing to bend over backwards (i.e. be meek and willing to go by the rules and get bashed over the head) to their detriment.

The animal is always willing to take advantage of any perceived weakness. Ruthlessness is just another practical view. Sick but very practical ... for an animal.

The real problem is that the human condition doesn't make sense. Until it does, neither stance can really make sense. The two features of practicality and dreaming must merge as we attain our humanity, our human nature. Practicality and dreaming should not be in conflict. They should not be considered mutually exclusive.

No more realists, no more dreamers, just humans. No more of any of the bizarre splits of which there are an endless array today.

There's an old saying, "Communism is the exploitation of humans by humans. Democracy is vice versa." I would only modify the phrase to read, "subhumans".

We have not fully inhabited the sentient state, so partial answers are all we ever find. We cannot accept our sentient state until we accept that there is something more to the sentient state: our human nature. We must admit that there is more than we ever imagined and where it originates.

We know it. We damn near froth at the mouth about it but we can't conceive the reality or what has always held us back from attaining it. We try early in life, in our innocence, to attain it. Then, as our innocence, honesty, and clarity become confounded by the delusions, we settle for less, either the vicious, ruthless animal or the hopeless dreamer.

We have been taught these lessons for millennia. It is no surprise that our existence is absurd. It's not even surprising, though it is striking, that we also *know* it is all absurd: existentialism at its miserable finest.

I wouldn't be surprised if the split between the dreamer and the realist align with those that find some way to find mutual pleasure and those that don't even try.

The terrible and sad truth is that we learn to accept our situation as if it is the best we should expect. It is all we have ever known. We know how horrible the absurdity is but we accept it as the best we can do. We completely miss the big picture, the primary reason we can't get resoundingly beyond the animal with no desire to look back. That makes me want to throw up all over again. It is nothing short of surrender. We should all be appalled.

The split personality drives us to extremes. Do we want progress, advancement at any cost or do we want a lotus position without the any complications? Do we wish to contemplate our navel or destroy anything in our path. Compromise remains a myth until the dreamer merges with the practical realist and we become human.

Both are distortions of the truth. Neither is human. We split between the two. There is a middle ground but we can't seem to find it.

Why does a stable, progressive approach escape our grasp? Because we are not a stable species - yet. Why are we not a stable species? Well, I've gone into that enough, haven't I? Dystopia is only the human condition, not human nature.

Elucidation

Truly, this chapter is only for those that are ready for it. It is for those that are not struggling with what I have already written. It is the most jumbled of my thoughts on the subject. They are new. No guarantees. If the previous readings were challenging, just skip right past this.

These thoughts have not been thought through, there is no clarity, but I think it senses a lot of the next step of understanding. It begins to connect all of the dots into a tapestry And, I'm *not* writing another friggin' book!

So, essentially, I hate the chapter myself but, still there's something here. That's probably why I hate it. I know I'll want to chase it down. If I do, if I make further clarity of it after the book is published, you'll find it on the website ... maybe ... or ask me.

I really wanted to start the book with this. But, it's not clear enough yet.

Some of this just seems really out there. If it gets too much for you, just jump to the next chapter. If you have had *any* trouble with earlier chapters, you should definitely skip right over this chapter to the next, Millennium. You are not ready for it.

I scoured the thesaurus to find the right word to describe this chapter. Elucidation is pretty darned close. There's one other word that seems closer but it is too well worn, too cheesy, and has too many connotations.

As I look deeper and deeper, the more I realize it had to happen this way. The accumulation of insights on multiple fronts were required for humanity, with two in particular.

Many fronts have always been paving the way towards clarity, the elucidation of reality, which is in fact maybe the best definition of human nature. You can call all of these fronts the ongoing search for clarity.

œ Because of human nature, because of our intellect, accumulated knowledge, awareness, curiosity, and creativity, we have always been on the path of seeking the truth. Or, in the vernacular of a sentient perspective: clarity. We seek any clarity, any truth, that stands up to every test. (That is why I am so baffled by the prolific, stupid, misinformation campaigns. These folks have committed to the animal).

We reveled in science over the last century because it could pin truth to the wall. Unfortunately, there are other truths, just as important, yet less scientific. Reducing life to a set of equations (or laws) constrains the view. There's more to life. Clarity at another level is required.

Truth in every form is very, very important to living a life with clarity, living within the domain of our human nature. Not remaining insane. We all seek truth and we all fall short because of one lie that rips through everything creating a snarl of lies and deceptions that are never-ending. It tripped us up from the start. Nothing is fine until that lie is gone.

When everyone can keep their balance because their balance has never been compromised, how difficult will it be to compromise that balance, that surety in life? Nearly impossible.

Emotional upheaval, maybe the worst trait of the human condition that leads to all of the havoc, is not genetic. It is induced by the failure to become human and stabilize and fulfill those emotions that complete our humanity.

Yes, survival will still overrule but, at this point in our journey, we have overcome the need to *only* survive. We need to succeed. The only reason some large populations still suffer threats to their survival is due to the narcissistic, limited animal version of survival that we have enacted as a race. It needs to be superseded by the *race's* survival needs and the survival of love.

That should be much more easily done, once the narcissism is gone. Narcissism is just another relic, another aberration, of the failure to make one from a population of two.

I'm not sure but I think that previous sentence may be the most insightful comment of a lifetime of seeking insights.

Wow! I think it explains a lot of what I have been trying to say.

When two people have the potential of really becoming one in every sense, things change. All of those selfish feelings will dissipate on the wind of love. But, you've had a handful of how bad I am at explaining, so I won't pick it further apart at this time.

You see what I mean??!! How do you take a simple statement like, "narcissism is a byproduct of two people remaining two" and explain it? Sheesh!

In essence, that is what I have been doing for a lifetime. Not purposely. In all honesty, I now look at my life and I'm kinda freaked out. I have been on a mission.

Over the last few years, I've been toying with this idea but I never took it terribly seriously. But, it's really beginning to freak me out. Really.

I've always left the door open to reincarnation. I know it's just another crazy idea that tries to make sense of afterlife. The other idea that is just as believable is an abyss of nothingness. Maybe the latter just doesn't appeal to me, I'm not sure. It's like the abyss of nothingness following this spectacular existence, just doesn't taste right.

Reincarnation became *very* attractive though, of course, not conclusive, as I studied its effects *in this life* further. I'm not one to delude myself and I know I don't know what's coming, but belief in reincarnation has ramifications in *this life*, your current instantiation of living.

The most powerful incentive that reincarnation induces is to *make things better in this instance of existence.* Even if it doesn't take effect until long after I am gone. The point is that reincarnation leaves the door open that *I could be back.* That is what really attracted me to the idea. It is the *only* afterlife that stirs an interest in what happens in this existence *before you are dead.* In other words, whether it works out that way or not, it induces a person to consider what happens to *this existence* after one is dead. You might just be back, so improvements that extend into the future are important.

Most religions just trash this existence, as if we were nothing more than an animal. The plan of every religion is to get the hell away from this life and never come back. That makes me violently ill.

Reincarnation invests the individual with some stake in what happens in this existence after one is dead. That seems a really good approach to this life.

Reincarnation does not rely on some god saving you from yourself or humanity from itself. We do that ourselves.

An instance from my life may better explain what I mean. I made a personal commitment because of an incredible woman that I adore. I committed to doing everything I could to make sure that, if we come back to this life, it would be a better place.

All of this and more drove me on to hit the note.

The drive to change things and study things in minute detail started from a very, very early age. So, I wonder if a previous me carried through its adamant desires into this life. I just have a difficult time otherwise understanding how I was so adamant that things were broken at such an early age.

We have been building an existence that has everything except for two crucial requirements in order for it to make sense: clarity and meaning regarding this existence.

We have been seeking truth in all things. We have been seeking clarity. We have been accumulating knowledge by the boatload with little certainty why. It has been just the curious nature of humanity at work.

On so many fronts, we have been seeking insights as if we were in a darkened room and feeling for the outlines. Maybe that's why the drooling misinformation babble-mouths annoy me so, so, so, *soooooooooo* thoroughly.

A big mistake I made in my earlier descriptions of this all was the belief that this could have happened earlier. In retrospect, that was just the annoyance that the burden fell on me. Why couldn't it have happened *before* I was born so that I could reap the rewards of being human rather than try to explain it to a bunch of twittereheads that while away their time.

This insight also has been growing in me. That, while the mechanics of men learning to love women physically are simple, it is progress on many fronts that was required. That's why it had to take so very long.

What is not so simple is all of the surrounding fronts seeking clarity. These fronts have been even sketchier than finally comprehending men's derailment of love and sex. It is almost like all of the other fronts had to drag these two out of the ditch. One front is explored silently while in bed with the lights out and the other in more poetry, song, and essays than can be named. And, yet, the twain never met. They would brush against each other in passing but remained unfamiliar to each other.

In countless songs, prose, poetry, instrumentals, every form possible, we have explored what little we understood about love.

In every form imaginable, except the one that counts, we have explored sex, the orgasmic pleasure, whether it included making it mutual or not.

The entangled lack found in the sexual experience that ensnared us pre-limited the potential of love.

Throughout these books, I have begged for women to understand what is really going on. And, again, it was a simplistic idea. The howling and growing fury of women is another important front in opening up the real layout of our predicament.

I finally realized that what the women really were saying has been, "Guys, there is something not right about you. We have no clue what it is but, please, figure it out." Unfortunately, the actual vernacular is closer to, "Get over yourselves." "Quit being toxically masculine!" While they are correct assessments, it really doesn't help at all, and the distortions and confusion just get worse. It probably kept us from blowing ourselves to kingdom come but never resolves anything. The problem, of course, is that men have obfuscated the problem and, thereby, all of their existence so thoroughly that women never had a chance of understanding.

It is like this tidal wave of fronts coming from every direction. From our desperate desire for love, from men's dissatisfaction with their situation, from women's dissatisfaction and misunderstanding of men's situation, from our senses, our perceptions, and our desire for clarity, perspective. It has *all* been necessary.

Essentially, there is this overall subconscious dissatisfaction of the species with our picture of existence in this universe that just won't shut up.

We have *always* been seeking the truth that gives this life meaning and it has been right in front of us. Just amazing!

Doubt

Men should not have the slightest doubt about their ability regarding coitus. Rather than being up to men to invariably fail at coitus, it should be up to the couple to succeed at love without that impediment. The onus is on the man to change the initial conditions and achieve the potential for coitus and relationships or, at least, not hide from it like a cowering animal. The male gender of the sentient species called human must step up to the plate and accept itself as man, not a male animal.

I look up into the stratosphere of those that can last a few minutes, which is far longer than I had ever lasted before. They must feel pretty good about themselves, right? They last a respectable period according to the two minute rule.

But, it has to stick in the craw of every man that the potential transcendent experience of coitus is just so far beyond men's seeming potential. Maybe it just takes longer to dawn on those that seem to be doing okay. I mean, they last longer than two minutes, so hooray!!! It is man's potential that we have disavowed - for no good reason. That's pretty weird. In fact, it's pretty crazy.

And, so on

You see what I mean? Messy, messy chapter. Sorry I couldn't do more. At least on this edit, it's almost beginning to make sense.

Millennium
Clarity

This really belongs in the previous section, but I didn't want you to miss it just because you remain baffled by it all and skipped the previous section in your denial.

The more I think on it, the more it becomes clear. Sentience is all about seeking clarity. Humanity has a depth of perspective on existence that so far exceeds the animal that it created something new, a desire for clarity due to the overwhelming awareness of sentience.

We have the ability to discern so much more than any other animal on the planet. Not just the rock in front of you or the stars in the sky but the nuances of existence that didn't even exist before humanity. Like the fact that animal coitus is incomplete. We can't avoid it, though we try so very hard to do so.

Sentient perspective seeks clarity. It is encumbered by distortions.

How do you think our desire for clarity performs when there is this gaping hole in our perspective regarding sex. Everything regarding sex has become so twisted. Our desire for clarity regarding sex has been blocked down through the ages by gibberish. That has made a hash of any attempt at overall clarity.

It makes sense. The last thing on Earth that early humanity should have had to question was sex. It worked. It did its job just the way that animals performed it. The idea that there was so much more hiding in plain sight was far beyond early humanity's ken.

Plenty of other quandaries remained baffling. Why even consider something that seemed so well understood and impossible to change? It was just too much.

I feel like I can almost see what happened. Coitus was important. It keeps the race from disappearing off of the map of existence. So, I can almost see someone asking why it is that men had all the fun and women just tolerated it. "That's just the way it is," would have been the dimwitted response of the animal ... and still is. "God made us that way," makes it all sound so predestined rather than just more gibberish. Just another useless answer that answered nothing.

"Coitus is for making babies. Any other thought is disturbed," was probably suggested by some woman that was tired of wasting her time with sex. At least the prospect of babies could keep her interest.

"Sex is cursed," was another big one. It kind of solved everything. It gave people an excuse to hate sex without ever realizing the real reason they hated sex.

It is all a misconception, wrapped in a lie, and carried along on the inertia of paradigms of nonsense and absurdity creating unending confusion.

One huge disturbance to our clarity sits right in the middle of humanity's existence and crushes our humanity.

We cannot become human until clarity is attained. We don't have a chance at clarity until we admit that we aren't even looking for clarity when it comes to sex and coitus. We have been bamboozled.

Clarity is the goal of sentient awareness.

Future

This chapter could be considered frivolous, and certainly should be considered cautiously. After all, it is the future I am pondering here. But, the long view (in both directions of time) is what allowed me to achieve the necessary insights, so I feel I must explore the future further.

Millennium

This section will *attempt* to concentrate on how mankind emerges into an unobstructed sentient state and, finally, expresses its human nature rather than its animal legacy. After all these long millennia of confusion, delusion, superstition, and deceit, what will our human nature actually look like?

This section is about the next thousand years. This is about glimpsing the future. What will we be like after one thousand years; as love, honour, dignity, grace and all of the finer qualities of our human nature finally have a chance to develop and flourish as sanity, emotional balance, and rationality begin to come to the fore, as clarity in the form of honesty regarding sex and coitus becomes the norm, and the fulfillment of the physical aspects of love become real?

The confirmation, the certainty of change should happen within a generation from whenever it begins. Substantial results should be apparent with one hundred years.

Even if we started today, I won't even see the first glimmerings of our human nature and clarity. Maybe that is one reason I wish to explore. I won't be around to see it, so I would at least like to attempt to get a sense of its glory.

Besides, I am sick of even thinking about the current horrific deluded state of humanity.

As a large proportion of humanity finally learns to love and begins to fill with self-respect that opens the floodgates to the finer qualities of a sentient existence, I am sure I will be in my grave. It ougtta be beautiful.

Yes, I'm equating love and our fully revealed sentience. More and more, they seem one and the same. Clarity and love may be the best description of the fulfilled sentient state. Loving coitus is just the vehicle to get us there. Clarity stands on it own. Loving coitus, though, seems the only way that I can determine that we attain the loving nature that is equivalent to our human nature. How can humanity attain fulfillment of love without loving coitus? I'm just not sure how that could happen. How is equality attained without women and men being equal in the loving endeavor of coitus? Rutting debunks love and, thereby, sentience *and* clarity. Clarity *might* be attained without loving coitus. Though a fulfilled loving state without loving coitus seems an oxymoron.

Our sentience has always recognized that there is something more to sex. We know it. Mutual satisfaction is paramount. Failing to do so crushes us. For a human, fulfilled coitus is the epitome of making love. Mutual satisfaction will go well beyond the bounds of sex, once coitus becomes a fulfilled human endeavor of making love, once two become one in a real sense. Mutual satisfaction (think the win-win of game theory) becomes a state of being.

Love can only begin to flourish amidst the most tremendous, transcendent sharing of a lifetime in the full sharing of pleasure face to face between man and woman. Not, "men take and women give...and give...and give." Sharing blossoms, propagates, and all the foolishness ends as men learn to give in the loving act of coitus. The nonsense ends abruptly.

Poof! We're sentient. How could it be otherwise?

So, what will happen in that first millennium? Love can become revealed in all its glory. It won't even take a hundred years, once we start, for humanity to see the truth of this.

While I'm hesitant to say I have discovered enough to assure that all men can succeed at coitus, I am absolutely certain that I have revealed enough to complete the journey. How long it will take us to complete that journey is the biggest unknown as to how long the road will be. In this contemplation of the events, I make the assumption that I am very, very close or right on the nose in The Real Kicker.

It may take a thousand years for love to be fully revealed in all its glory and fully reveal the magnificence of sentience and humanity. It starts with loving another and fulfilling that commitment of love between man and woman in bed. That is not where it ends.

It is difficult to explain the love I am attempting to describe because it hardly exists today. So far, it is just the sense of something grand and exciting that never really arrives. We have a sense but we have never really tasted it.

Just like innocence, love is not as it seems today. It is not a love that abandons rational thought. It is not a love that tolerates offenses. It is not a love that abases itself at the feet of another. None of those are love. The love between two that become one is also only the start of the journey.

That first instantiation of love between man and woman begins the fulfillment of the broader aspects of love that can commit to love others *that are worthy of love.* It only begins with the intimate relationship between two people.

As the race begins to mature, there will be more and more of those that are worthy of love and fewer and fewer of those that life derails and love finds wanting.

This love between two, this real instantiation of love, is an emotionally stable, rational love fulfilling our yet-to-be-attained emotionally stable, rational, and sane human nature.

Love and clarity will not tolerate excuses, deceits, delusions, or offenses, forgive obnoxious behaviour, and rationalize the beastly acts ("oh, they're only human"). A humanity that has fully attained its sentient state should not expect to encounter such or, at least, not often.

The real outlier that cannot be determined, since we have yet to meet any such, is alien intelligent lifeforms. I don't want to spend a lot of time with this subject but it keeps coming to mind and I must discuss it briefly.

I still maintain that an intelligent life-form that reaches the stars and a successful existence will be a loving, sentient race. One that doesn't will destroy itself. But, I also admit that could be my utterly optimistic nature coming to the fore.

The point I'm trying to make is that if we meet an alien life-form that is other than fully sentient and loving, it will not mean that we will turn the other cheek and get blasted into our constituent parts. It's not a love that rolls over and plays dead because someone has offended it.

Also, with the other 90% of our brain functioning, we will perform at our best, so we have our best chance of surviving anything, including an insane race that can't keep its eye on the ball.

No bets on whether we could overcome an insane race of alien beings, if presented with such. There are too many variables. There is just the surety that we will do our best if we are not deluded and wasting our time killing each other off.

That does not hone our skills. It just defeats us and displays that we are not yet more than a dimwitted animal or an incompetent sentient race, whichever way you choose to look at it. Enough on aliens that we may never meet.

The exciting result (to me, anyways) will be what men bring to the party of being human. Not only does men's bestial behaviour limit us. It also hides what lies ahead. The unique finer qualities that the male human that has become man will display, just like those which women have displayed for ages, will complement our sentient existence.

As I've mentioned before, many of what are perceived as feminine characteristics will prove to be human characteristics that are never displayed by the currently distorted version of the prehuman male.

I have no doubt that the fusion of the male and female spirit will be another staggering revelation but I won't even attempt to extrapolate that fusion. That potential is extremely difficult to trace at this point in time, since it does not yet exist. About all that can be said is that it ougtta be great. If by some miracle, I encounter the experience, you can bet I'll write another book explaining what I have learned.

The necessary discipline and forethought regarding coitus required to fulfill the man's role as a human, loving, sentient, emotionally balanced male are two of men's qualities that I expect to have a large impact. But, there may be others as men transform into something truly human.

The bliss of mutually gratifying coitus *should* be the bliss of life. It *should* be the greatest expectation of life fulfilled. The fulfilled, loving life of a human, fully sentient race puts paid on the misery and delusions of existentialism.

Another fascinating consideration is what will replace the seemingly impenetrable delusions, fictions of the animal, absurdity of nihilistic, narcissistic paradigms due to the liberation of 90% of our brains. Talk about revolutionary.

The liberation from all of the delusional paradigms that hold our minds hostage should be incredible but I have no gauge to even attempt to extrapolate what that will mean, other than humanity will finally be able to think clearly with a will.

This will be the start of the millennium in which we can finally acknowledge what we have known all along. Love is important and sex has a bad rep. Men being wholly human lifts us into our humanity, our sentience, and a clear understanding of love.

Three millennia versus one

How long will it take humanity to throw off *all* of the distortions introduced over three thousand years or so?

There's a lot to consider. While humanity may be able to change completely within one hundred years or three generations, it is difficult to determine how long it will take to abandon all of the nonsense and replace it all with something that makes sense. The *search* for clarity is only the beginning. There are a few factors that can be considered, though.

The human race regenerates constantly, which will be a big help. Some of those distortions, though, are institutionalized. How many can wither away in a single generation? Quite a few would be my guess. How many will fall by the wayside and how many will it take conscious effort to overcome?

Overcoming three thousand years of spouting nonsense seems like a lot to overcome but we'll save that for later.

It is the finer degree that is difficult to determine. As I've stated often, institutions, such as corporations, religions, and governments are really just groups of people. Are the organizational structures fatally flawed or is it just that they are populated by animals that look and act superficially like humans? Did the perverse mindset of the male influence the desire for hierarchical structure or is it really just the best organization? Will all of our existing ways of life work just fine once humans populate them? Or, do we need to overhaul everything we have created in three thousand years?

A sentient future

Sentience changed everything. The last few millennia have shown us what happens when we don't fulfill our sentient nature and, instead, remain too closely coupled to our animal ancestors' point of view.

We just never realized it. We realized only the small stuff, like we are really pretty smart. That we could make all kinds of toys with which to play. That we could destroy and offend with abandon. That something was wrong with our situation.

But, we missed the big stuff. Love. Honour. Truth. Dignity. Integrity. Clarity. These have all been swept aside by ignoring the tsunami of non-sentient sex.

The original blessing granted to humanity, Love, was lost for millennia. Its purest, initiating form, the physical love between two individuals, wasn't even a consideration. Once again, I have to admit that it wasn't lost, really.   It just wasn't ever found. We've been seeking it all along. It has just taken an awful long time to find.

If you look around at the proliferation of nonsense, it becomes obvious. Our wit was undermined by making excuses for lousy coitus rather than admitting the challenge. That started the ball rolling.

We could, then, be manipulated and bamboozled into believing that those people on the other side of the mountain were horrible monsters.   It created the perfect conditions for paranoia. We couldn't believe our own views since our self-respect never remained in tact.   So, we relied on some loudmouth with much less of a clue than the common human.

We didn't see those people on the other side of the mountain often and we certainly didn't get to know them, so it was easy for some power-seeking maniacal alpha male to grab hold of the animal's fear of the unknown, lack of surety in self, and convince all that *they* were the true light.

If you haven't noticed, it's happening, again.   It hasn't changed at all.   Just look at the misinformation channels and websites. Offensive, mindless fools, all of them.

Because we are the true light, we should go kill those other folks. They aren't really human or some such folderol. Right. Hitler for the 3rd Millennium. If it isn't clear, these guys can't last a few seconds. Bet on it. All because their willies go limp in short order and they can't face or compensate in a loving manner.

The real long view

I was just noting to myself how I have never focused on *less* than one hundred years. Most people cannot tune their focus beyond a quarter, if not a day into the future. In my case, I was so disgusted with the human condition, there was nowhere else to look.

Interestingly enough, we all look *backwards* many millennia.   But, how many really look?   How many take a sceptical look at all of the tomfoolery in our past rather than glorify it. The "good ol' days", whether they be yesterday or two thousand years ago, is all bullshit. How many look beyond the nonsense filling the history books about wars, heroes, godly decrees made by some human, and conflicts of every stripe that are nothing more than celebration of the animal?

Worse yet, how many look to those poor ignorant ancients for answers? There's a plan. They know sooo much more than us because ... ???

It's a matter of perceiving what was really going on rather than distracting ourselves with the big events that, in reality are nothing but minutiae, like wars, and egos, prophecies, messiahs, and messages of gibberish?

Do you notice how we have striven to achieve love since very long ago? It seems the simplest endeavor, but we never have achieved it. Instead, we morphed the meaning of love to suit our failures. We have always mistaken the small stuff for the big stuff and vice versa.

Love is the big stuff but, because of not reinventing coitus to suit humanity, it became distorted. Clarity has always been obscured. Paradigms of nonsense, the substitute.

We made a big thing out of Big Love, maybe in desperation, never realizing that without the successful accomplishment of the smallest, most intimate expression of love, the big stuff is only the stuff of dreams and delusions. Big Love cannot happen until the individual fulfills the intimate physical expression of love and becomes human and loving. How could it possibly be otherwise?

The dream flourishes when physical love flourishes. The delusions of love finally fade and we will know what all of love is really about.

One prediction that I become more and more confident in is that our progress should become breathtaking, once begun. It should capture our attention and never let go. Progress from our standpoint today may be difficult to recognize as it will change form so much and so rapidly from the brute force attempts at progress today.

I say this for a number of reasons.

Progress should be rapid because 90% of our brains won't be dealing with hogwash. We will be able to really think clearly and with purpose for the first time in our existence.

Also, as our emotional makeup becomes stable, we will be better equipped to determine what *needs* to improve *for the human race* rather than satisfy the urges of some greed-infested malformations of humanity.

Another consideration is how unabashed, unrestrained joy of life will affect the future. What happens when we can look forward without the nightmares that haunt us? A fully formed human tolerates no nonsense. How quickly will all of the nonsense be identified and how far is the toss into the bin? It can be measured in femtoseconds and nanometers for a fully sane, emotionally balanced human.

I am beginning to get so far away from the delusions we have forced upon ourselves that I have a difficult time focusing on what is so difficult about realizing that sentient coitus for a sentient species equates with love. Another reason I would rather concentrate on the future.

It is just so damned obvious to me, now. Mutual sharing of physical satisfaction initiates love. Honestly? I have to believe there are some women out there saying, "Duh!" Women were never the impeding factor and a few must have avoided the delusions and distractions provided to the extent that they can see through to that truth. Many find that mutual satisfaction, one way or another. That is a start.

Love, a higher form of caring than an animal can ever attain, cannot fully exist without sentient coitus, though. Anything else is half measures. Completely replacing coitus with test tubes makes me physically ill.

Where do we go from here?

I finally got one answer for that which I was future-seeking, because I finally found the right question in order to answer the other question: what happens next? As humanity gains its balance, what happens?

The right question to ask, in order to seek an answer to that question is: what happens when humanity finally gains self-confidence and, thereby, self-respect? What happens when each human being has respect for and confidence in themselves and, *then*, all of humanity? The latter can't happen overnight. There will be a lot of human animals roaming around for a some while, so the confidence in humanity may take a little while.

Men have never been fully confident due to what I've been discussing throughout four books. Their self-respect turns to ashes as they reach puberty. It just gets worse from there. Women, well, women have had their legs knocked out from under them (double-entendre) since way before sentience ever existed.

What actually led me to the right question was pondering the paradox of paradigms. Paradigms are useful. It would be difficult to live without them. Yet, they are also a bane on the current human condition.

We are fed paradigms of nonsense from the time we are born, both by actions and attitudes (sometimes referred to as osmosis, that circumvents the thought processes entirely) as well as words, well before our critical faculties develop as a defense against nonsense. The worst paradigms are those that we pick up by osmosis. These burrow so deep you don't even notice how they sway you. They are seldom questioned. To make it even worse, it is declared they have to be taken on faith. Right. They are taken as fact, even when assaulted with sense. Hence, my difficulty getting through to a brain that is 90% dysfunctional and filled with nonsense.

In general, we don't even attempt to do anything about this nonsense we absorb as kids because we aren't consciously aware of the absurdity of it all. There is no questioning the veracity of the nonsense. Instead, a lot of the paradigms act as a salve for our bestial condition as well as reinforcing it. We are so discombobulated that we don't question what is clearly utter nonsense.

It's like looking at your shadow. It's there and there's nothing to be done about it. "We're only human", blah, blah, blah. As the discrepancies build up in life, as the deceits become more obvious, we just crumble under the burden of lies. Bitterness is the usual result which, of course, seeks to find someone, something to blame.

Each individual crumbles under the burden of a fractured view of our existence typified by the paradigms like "we're only human", "love all" (even if you're not prepared to do so and humanity is not prepared to accept it), "it's not personal", or, maybe my favorite "it's just sex".

The paradigms rule us, not the other way around. That's when it dawned on me that we let the nonsensical paradigms rule us. Ruling our paradigms may be a big part of what will occur over the next few centuries as clarity burns through the nonsense. It is that burning outrage I mentioned at being fooled that will disallow nonsensical paradigms from ruling us. They won't get in the door.

One reason paradigms rule us is that we have no confidence in ourselves as individuals or as a race of sentient beings. Our self-respect and confidence have been continually ground into dust, obliterated before they have a chance to develop. We replace clarity with paradigms of nonsense because they take no thinking and they satisfy the animal.

We even have paradigms to cover our incompetence as a sentient race. Original sin and so forth. We are screwed before we get started. Right.

We don't trust ourselves, so we accept all of the nonsense. We consider ourselves nothing but an overly smart animal that is doomed to fail.

We wave our hands around, discuss how terrible humanity is and hope some nebulous being will save us rather than saving ourselves. We fiddle while Rome burns.

As the belief in the credibility of those gods fade, the animal's ruthlessness has become even more of a factor.

That's big. That's the change that gives a good indication of where we will be going once we abandon the nonsense, and where we will end up if we don't. We let the paradigms rule us because we are used to doing things that way and we have had no confidence or enough self-respect to change anything or refute the nonsense. We let some god that some human created, or some ruthless lunatic ruler and laws guide our actions rather than relying on humanity's stability, rationality, and sanity to rule. The most ruthless and stupid embrace anarchy and manipulation of the existing systems for their own benefit. They perceive the moral guidelines as something to be trampled for their narcissistic benefit.

The implications of humanity gaining its self-respect and confidence reaches into every aspect of our future existence.

Fear

Today, we rule and are ruled by fear. It makes me sick when I see how those fears are played upon (think misinformation and stupid people that profit from it).

The delusions are nothing new. It is still that the people on the other side of the hill don't do things the way we do, so they deserve to be blown up. It doesn't really matter what they do differently or how different they look, the most feeble-minded will find some way to justify blowing them up. Misinformation and conspiracy theories are based on hate and begin with self-hate and hate for the human race.

Many would rather see the whole Earth turned to ashes than admit they are so very wrong. That's not new, either. Just the weapons of destruction are. This time, the fall would really, really hurt. Did you know that nuclear weapons are on the up-tick again?

I won't be around to see the outcome. All I can do is hope that our wit exceeds our delusions, paradigms of nonsense, vanity, ruthlessness, and destructiveness, thus allowing us to finally see the way forward as a sane, stable, loving, sentient race before we do something utterly stupid and dive off the cliff unknowingly, which is our usual method as we drown in our stupour as the cycle repeats. I hope that 10% of the brain is enough to see through.

There is really one fear I have that is worse than that. That humanity, in its utter stupour, would rather go down in flames than ever face the truth that humanity can be magnificent. It seems so deeply ingrained to be horrified by the idea that humanity can be great.

It seems to set off alarms almost as loud and insistent as any thoughts regarding sex. God will strike you down for the hubris of thinking you could be as great as some fictional being that some butt-scratching animal dreamed up thousands of years ago.

It would be hubris to think that sentience *and* coitus are good things. Right? That there is so much more to each than we ever suspected.

One hundred years

It is most likely that a significant portion of the change will be obvious in less than a hundred years from the time it starts. I won't even see it begin.

That's the doom of a real strategist, not some economics major in the Finance department. I'll consider myself lucky to see it even begin to catch on that we can be more than just an animal. I'll consider humanity lucky if it ever begins. I've done what I could but I'm not too impressed with my efforts.

In less a hundred years, a species can be transformed into a race of beings that can bear the title of sentience with honour, integrity, dignity, confidence, and self-respect. In a hundred years, a race can transform itself from a grubbing, ruthless animal and begin to learn all about self-respect, love, innocence, and all of the noble qualities of a sentient race.

A sentient race can learn to quit using the terms awareness, intelligence, sentience, and honour, integrity, dignity, self-respect, love as if they were dirty words. Then, we can begin to explore sapience.

The really long game

I'm done with the past and the first one hundred years into the future.

I've mapped out how humanity can transform itself. I've detailed the cause of our insanity ad nauseam. I have led the jackass to water. I have detailed how it will probably take one hundred years (i.e. three generations) to fully realize the potential of love. I've made significant breakthroughs in what it takes to make coitus into a loving engagement.

I can't force the change. I can only point out what is needed and have done so. I'm not going to wait patiently for humanity to catch on. I don't have that kind of time or patience.

So, it's time to turn to an even longer timeframe and, then, I'm really done with this subject. A single millennium sounds about right. If humanity can't get it right from what I have delineated, there's nothing more I can do regarding the shorter term ... or, at least, nothing more I am willing to do.

I am going to do my damnedest to stay focused on the longer term of one thousand years for the rest of this book but, since I do not feel like even the one hundred year perspective has gained any traction through the existing three books, I will probably attempt to clarify further as I go. In other words, I'm afraid I will digress some. It is all rather intertwined. And I'm *not* writing another friggin' book!

This is no longer just connecting the dots, but filling in the colors to some extent as well. Also, there always seems more I can convey about our absurd situation and *its* demise ... or ours. I'm just exhausted from the effort and the lack of response. Stupid humans. Since it is the last time I will write on the subject, I shall indulge myself.

Focusing on what could happen over a thousand years really changes the thought processes quite a bit and feeds back to the one hundred year perspective, as well. I'm not quite sure how to approach it, yet, but, it is interesting. A thousand years. That's a lot of time for change once beneficial change is consciously sought.

A thousand years is more than enough time to gain solid footing and follow the path of unobstructed sentience to sapience. It will no longer be a question of what happens once we get there. Sometime before the end of that timeframe, it will become a question of what a sentient race can do once it gains its sapient potential, as well. Beyond that point is well above my pay grade.

I think this also explains my four previously published books (three that remain published) and my method of writing. I write things down to clarify for myself. I write it down for the purpose of consideration to see if I can poke any holes in it (which explains the multiple books worth of verbiage written from my previous forty years that were never worth publishing).

Only then, when there are no holes to be found, do I try to put it in terms that others may read in order to gain perspective. I'm afraid that has tended to make the writing a bit messy. Sadly, the heavily deluded (which seems everyone) consider it a chance to pick apart rather than attempt to consider it seriously. I hope I have done a little better this time around.

Hey, you try reversing the friggin' direction of insanity, vanity, and absurdity of a race that has dragged its animal roots around with it for three thousand years!

Then, have some fool react in a knee-jerk manner spewing the nonsense that it has absorbed without any real thought. I spent fifty years figuring out what is wrong with humanity and some fool spouts some version of the paradigms of nonsense that they learned at their daddy's knee back at me. Yeah, that always makes my day.

Crystal ball

Being able to experience love, innocence, and honour, etc, may, in fact, open up whole new vistas that are only available for study through the lens provided by those qualities and emotional fulfillment.

I'm guessing my accuracy will not be worth a fig after about five hundred years. No problem. By then, we will have succumb to the animal or transcended it, completely. If we transcend the animal, it may be fun for those generations to decide how accurate I was. If we continue to succumb to the animal, it won't matter. In that case, it is highly likely we will be extinct much sooner than five hundred years.

At first, I was going to say that within one hundred years my suggestions regarding the future would be faulty but, even if the changes inherent in attaining our sentience by learning to love were to begin today, I rather think the next couple of hundred years are rather straightforward. The time will be spent adjusting to the new circumstances and perspective, relegating more and more nonsense into the bin, and, of course, reveling in the astounding reality of love.

At some point, though, the change in perspective will begin to make a huge difference. We will mostly stabilize as we seek our way further. Further crucial insights will probably take quite awhile, unless they are concomitant to the fulfillment of the promise of love.

Two to five hundred years seems about right for something of such significance to occur to derail my future scenarios to some extent. It will take full comprehension and comfort with this current adjustment before anyone will be able to make further radical breakthroughs, if there are any to be made. I can't think of a thing that can hold a candle to loving coitus as a crucial change. But, then again, I was only raised to be an animal.

Also, I may not be accounting well enough for the effect of freeing 90% of our brain to think. I have absolutely no gauge for that. The possibilities are staggering.

No worries

This future I am attempting to portray is not about revolution. It is about evolution of consciousness. As such, it will be a gentle change. We won't need to force change because we will be so caught up in becoming human that minor adjustments, like how we organize, will fall out of the adjustments of becoming human. Revolution has always been a fool's errand.

Even though we face a discontinuity regarding the foundation of our existence (split infinity), it is not the sort that can cause upheaval. It is just the fruition of what we have always sought. It is the sort of change that will prevent upheaval and replace it with a steady hand.

Any change to the day to day activities of being human will be a long time coming. It will occur as a ground swell of *human* effort. That pegs it at about one hundred years. It will, initially, just be a change in the tone of activities.

I can use my own life as an example. I went from an individual that flowed through life with little concerns, but a lot of questions, to one that was so shocked by what I had discovered that it placed me into personal upheaval for a period of years - not decades. The decades of upheaval was due to - well, you should know by now.

This was replaced by an even more serene view as I realized that all of the absurdity of our current existence will wash away with the changing tide. It is not a permanent state. That really is the point.

My current agitation has to do with whether anyone else is ever going to put away their own delusions and nonsense in order to become human, not with the change itself.

What happens next? It's kind of exhilarating to consider, really. If you can't tell, I am very tired of the butt-scratching animal. Mostly, they just piss me off.

We *can* change. I consider it near certainty that we will change, even while I chafe at the delay. I am not the first to seek answers to our insanity and absurdity. It has happened repeatedly throughout our history. Simone de Beauvoir, Freud, Sophocles, Christ, Buddha, Emerson, The Flower Power generation, chivalry, are just a few attempts to break through.

This gives me further confidence that we have always been directed towards something better than the miserable existence that we have so easily accepted. The tsunami has been building for a long time.

It's just that I am the first to see the big picture with some clarity (no false humility there!). Even if my attempt to bring clarity fails, we are already on the road. Let's just hope we last long enough for someone to explain it better than me or, better yet, a few people can get past my inept writing and get what I am saying.

We have been avoiding the one and only issue that inhibits our ascendence into a sentient state in the most bizarre fashion. But, still, it is all moving in the right direction. If we don't blow ourselves to smithereens first.

Cracked crystal

The funny thing is how the portion of humanity that seeks our ascendence never seems to accept how awful and destructive the most animal portion of humanity can become. When it hits full force, they either don't seem to see it coming or watch helplessly as their fears become reality.

One thousand years

Something about that really inspires me. One thousand years. It really gets the thoughts flowing!

There is a tremendous amount of change that can happen in a thousand years. And, this time, the change can be purposeful and aimed in a direction that makes human life more human - rather than less so.

It's kind of amusing to see the fear of AI. We already allow our machinery to rule us and it is all leading the wrong way. Yes, AI is dangerous as long as we are.

Retrospective

Maybe this growing state of retrospective I am feeling is the place to start on a millennial view.

An interesting one for me has been pondering my writing. Writing precisely what I meant to say was impeded. I think about that missing 90% of the brain and the delusions that hijacked it. I think about the clarity that we pursue. I think about all of the gibberish we accept in place of clarity. It all makes me believe that precise communication will become the norm and crucial. With the end of nonsense and recovery of 90% of our brain, it should not even be too difficult.

As we put paid on the nonsense and credulity, we will be able to think more clearly and, thus, convey what we mean more precisely. We will quit avoiding reality. Clarity and precision grade thinking go hand in hand. I'm not sure how to weave that into the view of the future. It seems important, somehow, but far beyond any summary I can describe.

As I read through any book now, I am struck by the acceptance of our less than desirable state. I am currently reading *David Copperfield* and *The Cat Who Walks Through Walls* and I think about all of the many, many, many books (literally thousands) I have read.

Throughout everything I read or otherwise encounter, my perspective gains momentum as it continues to hold true against the backdrop of our needs, desires, and current inhuman condition of distractions, delusions, absurdity, credulity, and nonsense. It all reinforces the animal. It is all just a matter of accepting our state as if there were nothing to be done about it. Everyone settles. Everyone seems quite content with viewing humanity as an animal and seeking their own little vicious victories as if they meant something.

Maybe the best concept to cover our current situation is that we are not self-actualizing as a race. If you are not familiar with the term, it is a psychology concept in which a person basically says, "I can do better than this, dammit!" (at least that's my interpretation of it). We have convinced ourselves that we can't do any better, so we grasp at straws and call them "better".

I have been plagued with the concept of self-actualization for as long a I can remember. What made it a plague was that *I wasn't just considering myself.* Self-actualization is the natural human state when unimpeded. Right now, we wallow in nonsense instead.

I have always believed that *humanity* can do better, dammit - in no small way. I have always been convinced that humanity is more than a dense animal with only the wit to make itself miserable, cause others unlimited pain, and wholesale destruction, dammit! It all has to do with awareness and clarity.

I also finally accepted the fact that men are the problem (or, more exactly, men's limp willy). I'm rather convinced I was always aware of this. I just never admitted it. It's not politically correct. I mean, it is so very obvious. How did we miss it?

Sure, there were plenty of wild goose chases throughout my pursuit of what is wrong with humanity's condition. But, it is certain that I never ever accepted that men were acting in a human manner.

40,000 feet

Consider those previous forty years, before the last decade in which clarity began, as a view from forty thousand feet. In retrospect, it was probably crucial that I always defaulted to a hundred year perspective.

Any less and I would have been grubbing into the horrible mentality of Wall Street or scifi authors, willing to think that success with money, no matter how ruthless or wasted it made me, was really success rather than an affront to my human nature.

Any longer and I would have missed the critical point that we can make a significant change now, not at some distant point in some vague future because we've invented the perfect laws and guidelines to tell us how to *act* human (I went down that road far enough to realize it led nowhere). If I had been interested in my success and focused on a thousand years, I probably would have written a lot of vague, non-pertinent science *fiction*, with lots of action and drivel.

Nature created us fully equipped to *become* human. We just have to realize it.

I guess one of the events in my life that illustrates this is my reading of speculative fiction, usually in the form of sci-fi. Even in the scifi pertaining to the most distant future, humanity is still represented as the grubbing, miserable creature that it is today ... or a big brain being fed by tubes. That always bothered me. Somehow, that seriously upset me. It just didn't make sense. It was an incongruity that always rubbed me the wrong way.

Well, credit where credit is due. There is a woman (she knows who she is). She's got a dark side. She bit hard on the belief that humanity is a horrible mess, that there is nothing to be done, and one should take what one can get. She bled on the altar of our inhumanity a very long time. She kinda revels in the darkness. I hope that's over.

I could never ever understand the dark view at all. Inadvertently, one might even say, unknowingly, she helped me understand. As I guess you can tell, I never went dark. Funny thing, my thoughts on her have never changed. 220 volts, through and through. I like it. I just hope she gains the peaceful state of mind that will unleash everything that she contains, restrains.

Maybe people fear the idea of becoming fully sentient because they fear it would become boring. To me, it seems intuitively obvious that it will be anything but boring. I don't think I want to digress so far as to explain why but, maybe this will do. Loneliness, lethargy, and boredom are remnants of the beast, remnants of needing validation.

I really don't want to go backwards and review or repeat what I have already written but, once again, I am staggered by the fact that women seem to rebel at the idea that they are *not* a fundamental part of the problem, that it is men's failure that is the fundamental component that is disrupting our existence.

It's very sentient of women, really. Women have always been willing to take on the burden selflessly. Unfortunately, when dealing with an animal, sentient manners don't work so well. Informed, armoured innocence is required. We can drop the armour once humanity becomes human.

40,000 miles

I am trying my damnedest, in this section, to move my perspective to a forty thousand mile level, with little success. I have done all I can from the hundred year perspective. It is time to move on, dammit. But, it is difficult.

The mental difficulty of changing my perspective to one thousand years is a frustrating challenge.

This distant future perspective doesn't play to my strengths, the strengths that have been honed over most of my life and, especially, the last decade. I'm not really sure how to correlate and connects dots that don't yet exist. It is a quandary. The dots become too vague and insubstantial.

I've always used the analogy of connecting the dots as the discovery process I have used to comprehend what is wrong and how to fix it. Because of the massive amount of obstruction from paradigms it really was like walking around blind and feeling my way (the intuitive bent of my poetry helped vastly).

In actuality, though it was more like I collected so many dots that the picture finally appeared. That essentially ripped apart the veil of delusions and it all, then, became very, very clear. It has just been hard to elucidate to others. All intuition and no words.

All of this vague pondering may seem like it ought to be deleted (the thought crosses my mind regularly). But, there is a purpose to leaving it.

I think it's pretty clear that my mind works differently. I am hoping some of it will rub off. Yeah, there's that lack of humility, once again. ;~j

Altogether, I'm prevaricating and digressing like mad.

Perspective

So, I guess, as an alternative, I am going to use the audience as a silent participant in this effort to change perspective. It sounds crazy but, if you haven't figure it out by now, I am all about entertaining crazy thoughts in order to find insights and resolution to relieve our messy, miserable, dystopian existence.

The Basics

Maybe it will help to start with the basics. As we progress into our sentient state unfettered by the fundamental delusions and deceptions regarding sex, it is certain that our ability to think will become less burdened with nonsense. My own estimate is that will be the biggest change. The increasingly stable emotional outlook is crucial, also. Clarity and rational thought will begin to prevail. I consider those given. I just don't know how to estimate the effects of such drastic changes.

How can the ability to use our mind unburdened not change everything drastically? Another factor for which I cannot begin to estimate its impact is clarity. It is like the certainty of self-respect and confidence personified.

Stupefaction is replaced with thinking. Cowering in delusions is replaced with a laser sharp perspective on what is really going on. Outrage at nonsense rather than acceptance. I tremble at the implications and fear I will sell it all short because the reality goes far beyond even my wild, unconstrained imagination. How powerful can our existence be once the stupour ends, once the fabrications cease, once our sentience steps forward?

Think also of the emotional stability replacing the instability. I begin to see why I am hesitating. It is very frustrating. The reality will so far supersede anything I can describe as to make it feel a waste of time. I ache with every fiber of my being to see the reality. All of the words I have written on the future, after further consideration, seem paltry.

Absurdity

I still struggle with how relationships will evolve. Is there really such a thing as a "special fit", a soul mate? Or, will we find that just about any pairing will do?

It seems like the whole idea of a soul mate is just another example of our misinterpretation of love. It is seeking validation in another and accords for men an excuse for never finding it.

The gauge

Something I have struggled with throughout the time I have been exploring the nuances of the debacle we have endured is how long will it take for humanity to right itself, to just finally get on its feet. I've pegged it at, generally, on the order of one hundred years. This is, of course, dependent on how close I have been to reversing failed coitus. While I expect there to be further, possibly huge, improvements, I think I have set the basics out well enough to succeed and proceed.

We certainly cannot expect to reach a steady state of sanity and clarity in ten years and it cannot take one thousand years to hammer the nail home, once we admit it exists. The complete renewal of the species every hundred years or so seems to peg it well at around a century.

So, one hundred years will do as an estimate for attaining the essence of our humanity. What does that mean, though?

It certainly does not imply that we have reached a human condition that is equivalent to our human nature. I truly doubt we will have put away *all* of the nonsense in one hundred years. But, we should have been able to put away the most damaging, the most offensive, most egregious, blatant examples of our delusions and other nonsense.

One hundred years should be, at least, the state in which humans have redirected their efforts to attain their human nature, have the essentials in place and, at least, begin pondering the wonder of our humanity in depth. We will, at least, know intimately that we are seeking clarity for our sentient perspective in all things.

Maybe it will be like a great deal of the clamour and noise of our existence will be toned down in one hundred years. All of the finer human qualities should be displayed prominently. By then, it should go well beyond timid, tentative expressions of our human ascendency and far away from the rattle and bang of today. Outrage at the noise of the animal should begin.

Quiet might descend as we begin to really understand how different humanity is from the animal and the awful conditions we have endured. It seems like the shock and awe of the realization of our humanity should make us pause. If humanity is not awestruck, I will be very, very surprised. I am becoming convinced more and more so. Split infinity.

I will put the onus on the generation that really begins to see with clarity to succinctly explain the differences from today. Only that generation will be able to distinguish clearly enough. They are the only ones that will see the split infinity clearly in both directions. I so wish I was around to read it.

Maybe that's not entirely true. The document trail of our current nonsense is well recorded on Twitter and Facebook, news websites, and the drivel spouted by those that use religions or politics to make their millions. The politicians, though, are just much better at covering their trail. Maybe it will be easier to discern by later generations than I think.

But, basically, there is only one generation that will go through the dramatic event of clearly seeing the mess from which they have emerged and the tremendous vista that our future displays: our transcendence into human. More and more, I wish I could be there.

I would expect nothing less than an overwhelming desire to accelerate our change into something human.

This is making a lot of sense. We have avoided inspecting ourselves for far too long. It is time that we do some serious self-inspection until it is all well understood. I'll leave that war to you. I've already been there. I cleared the path.

I want to set the target at one hundred years for a moment, or the point at which the dreamer and the practical merge into one and clarity begins to emerge as a force with which to reckon. I am a dreamer through and through (does it show?). Since I've been pondering the next level, I've tried to look at things from a more balanced perspective. I've failed miserably. I cannot determine what is practical and what is only a dream. I will always default to the dream.

What I'm driving at is that I think that the more stable people of a century hence will not have such difficulties. They will be far more confident in their own determinations than I ever could be. They will be far more comfortable being a practical dreamer seeking clarity. Merging the practical and the dreamer could be defined as my underlying motive always. I could always see both sides. The practical side leans too much to the narcissistic, clearing its path with self-indulgent paradigms. The dreamer side leans too much to the previously blurry-beyond-repair hope of attaining our sentience leaning too much to a vague dream. My fondness for the dream is probably evident in those words.

Still, the condition of sanity and clarity in which a sentient perspective of reason, clarity, and emotional stability reigns unopposed is a far cry from having righted all of the damage done to the integrity of our cultural structure.

If there is one thing I have learned over the lifetime of a strategist is *everything* takes time. *Sigh*. I'll peg the former at two hundred years (it could be as short as fifty years) from the get-go. The latter really could take five hundred years or longer. The practical dreamer will be seeking clarity for about one to two hundred years. The next three hundred or so will be intentional restructuring towards what clarity has surmised.

I say five hundred years for a lot of reasons. I tend to think in term of eastern health insights when I think of healing. A really cool guy from Singapore that I once knew rather well, suggested that the eastern view of one returning to a healthy condition requires just as long as one was unhealthy. I don't think that is the exact wording but the essence is there. So, that would say it would take *four thousand* years or more for humanity to reach a "healthy" state, reversing all of the damage.

The damage to our 'health', by my estimation, began about four thousand years ago. Before that, for all intents and purposes, humanity was just a dumb animal. I peg it at about the time we began to express ourselves seriously. I can still remember reading some gibberish by a pre-Socrates authors. They were nuts. They were seriously whacked. Really. Gibberish. Before that, we might as well have been animals.

I often think that ancient Greece was as good as it got. After that, we quickly became burdened with nonsense. At that time, it was all new, refreshing. Then we got bogged down in minutiae and absurdity, distraction and deceit, trapped into the delusions as we remain today.

Compensating for the four thousand year span, though, is that this fulfillment of our humanity will be done with intent to improve or not at all. The last four thousand years have been an animal's mongering. It should be easy to overcome.

For the last four thousand years, we have, essentially, just piddled. The past four thousand years were just wallowing around in the befuddled muck of the animal, haunted by our animal heritage, with no clearly stated intent or purpose.

So, five hundred years to rid ourselves of the baggage that the animal carried along and forced into every niche of the human condition with insane maunderings.

For four thousand years, amidst the ongoing query of the human being of "why" the answer was the animal's reply of "because I said so". Usually portrayed as a thunderous voice of some god shaking the Earth with idiotic words. And, of course, honour thy parents because they have such a great grip on reality. It's just amazing to me how people will listen closely if some fool claims the nonsense he spouts comes from some god.

We will begin to treat all others with respect and the good will that they *deserve* just because it is the sentient thing to do rather than because it is politic, whatever the hell that means.

If we don't react purposefully regarding the existing human condition, as a single entity, without factions proclaiming some nonsense, within two hundred years, I will be spinning in my grave. Heck, I'll probably be spinning *until* we react with prejudice against any existential offense to human nature.

How long will it take for the layers of absurdity to be shed and our human nature to proliferate into every aspect of the human condition? I guess, for now, I have to say within two hundred to one thousand years? I'm leaning more and more towards the two hundred year end of the spectrum. The unencumbered brain, driving intent, clarity, and determination to get out from under the animal may even make it sooner.

The next step is obvious but still vague. After we have stabilized our condition into something completely human, what do we do next? Sapience. It seems almost the natural outcome, the evolutionary next step.

Some (very little) of the scifi I've read (and there's been a lot of that) seems to apply, maybe. I think of those stories of becoming extremely industrious and applying a methodical progress using rational argument seems about right. I just haven't a clue exactly what industriousness will be in order. In what direction(s) does a fully functional humanity delve? The advancements in science and technology could be beyond our comprehension. Or, we could take off in a completely different direction, for all I know. Well, whatever, it should be spectacular. The singularity may be just us.

I am certain that, once we gain momentum, it will be an exciting time of expectant change. Idiocy should be left by the wayside in short order. Only the first generation, the generation that did not grow up with the realization, will imprint the slightest grudging attitude on the change that will be nothing short of spectacular. After that, it should be pure enthusiasm and realism. Once men learn they can love, there is nothing holding us back.

Star level

Finer measurements and love

That brings me to the pubescent generation, as the change begins. When they get ahold of this they should be able to run with it. It could look a lot like the Flower Power generation, just less drugs and much, much, much more sense. "Free Love", that turned out to be nothing more than rutting sex with strangers, will be transformed into a thoughtful respect for the word Love, its physical manifestation, and the beginnings of a deep understanding of all of its ramifications and constituent parts.

I wonder, now, though, if there aren't further implications regarding love that I can't even begin to suggest.

Everything in me tells me there is so much more to love than I suspect. That I am like a blind person attempting to sense a rainbow. Maybe that is intuition or just hopeful gibberish.

We have a lot to learn about that particular word, love, especially once it is soundly connected to the physical act that brings it forth. Each reinforcing the other and bringing it to depths unknown (double entendre unintended).

Consequences

The real point of the preceding discourse has to do with how an unleashed sentient being (and race) will engage life.

I keep stumbling upon the same point. A huge difference will be that we *won't* revert to the violent animal's unreasoning hate and disruption at the drop of a hat (or economy).

Today, many avoid becoming an automaton by throwing away the essence of their humanity. Some fools call it recognizing reality (rather than the truth). In actuality, it is succumbing to the brainless common denominator of the animal. That bizarre perceptions are reality. All mouth and no brain.

Let me put that into context for you. "Perceived" reality is the reality of a sentient being deluded into accepting a non-sentient, offensive existence. "If you can't beat them, join them." Right. There's a plan. Practicality in the extreme.

As we become human, it will be the exact opposite. We will avoid becoming an automaton by fiercely protecting our finer qualities, starting with the self-respect and self-confidence that is no longer disabled and corrupted in youth.

Retaining one's self-respect and confidence won't be difficult at all. It is only recovering them that is difficult. The biggest issue will be identifying all of the broken human condition traps of the animal strewn throughout our existence. How quickly does our sense of truth, honesty become unquestioned? How quickly and thoroughly do we rid ourselves of the offenses against our *human* nature?

Does it take a long time to slog through all of the existing nonsense like landmines or do they become as obvious as a neon sign to our unimpeded senses and overwhelming desire for clarity, almost like a radar that senses an aberration from far away? I'm betting on the latter. The fog will give way.

So, the question would then become, once we sense clearly all of the stupidity surrounding us, how long will it take to unravel and dismantle the absurdities?

The adjustment from living the advanced life of a highly evolved, destructive, frustrated animal into that of a fully functional sentient entity will be no small change. It shouldn't be difficult because our hearts will be in it. But, it will take a lot of adjustments. Huge adjustments. It will certainly take, at least, one hundred years. Two hundred seems more likely.

But I am the utter optimist. And, I don't trust that optimism in this case (or any other, for that matter, amidst so much nonsense). I really don't feel like scrutinizing to the same extent that was necessary to reveal what it will take to finally attain our humanity. Fifty years of effort is enough for me. I'll leave further scrutinization to someone else. Fifty years!

I feel like I'm seeing it more clearly. It will be like previous generations, such as the Flower Power generation but with clarity and a specific goal in mind. We will fight fiercely to attain our humanity, once it is revealed that the fight no longer seems hopeless. Sadly, I'll have to leave that war to you, also.

The problem today, that I think I've described in good enough detail already, is that self-confidence and self-respect is damaged beyond recognition before a person even gets their feet under them, before they self-actualize and develop their reasoning faculties.

The huge adjustment for the first generation is this: overcoming the paradigms of nonsense that are adopted before the sentient faculties developed. That shortens or extends the timeline for overcoming the nonsense. I am rather certain that will take no more than a single generation. A generation that reaches puberty accompanied by success at loving (in whatever form) should be able to overcome the nonsense instilled during their childhood without difficulty, thus not passing it on at all to the next generation.

From there, full awareness of truth makes for fierce protection of truth. It becomes a personal thing. It becomes protection of one's own self-respect and confidence bolstered by a degree of clarity.

Generations have always rebelled for a reason. It is that sense of truth, that search for clarity, that rebels. It is beaten out of each generation thoroughly from pubescence on.

Until the unvarnished truth becomes obvious, though, it remains just thrashing around in the dark. The rebellious desire for clarity that makes generations rebel was always infiltrated by the lie before they ever got a good start.

Our reasoning has always been assaulted by an unstable emotional state, with the individual's self left in tatters by the mid-twenties to early thirties at the latest.

Information that we accrued, as something more than an animal but less than a human, wrecked our traditional innocence, our witless innocence of an animal.   Informed, armoured innocence has to take into account the mass of misinformation that humanity accrued *and the accurate information that was buried as if no one would notice.*

I guess informed innocence is all about that sense of truth and clarity that has been so bent out of shape over the millennia. It is about being able to rely on that senses of awareness, truth, and clarity.

We caved on informed innocence and that sense of truth about four thousand years ago. "Knowledge is dangerous. Let's revert to the animal."   "And, ***don't*** think about sex!"   This all just emphasizes what I have repeated ad nauseam.   There's no middle ground.   Either we become human or we continue to mimic a sick, awful representation of a human.

I think of the myths of Pandora's Box and The Garden Of Eden that were developed long ago.   It becomes even clearer than before that the former attempts to explain the confounding aspects of existence for a newly minted sentient being. Pandora's Box was the most honest exploration of what was going on.   The latter, the Garden Of Eden is so full of the sickness of corrupted innocence, intentional misinformation, shame and blame, that it makes me ill even to ponder it.   That pegs the destruction of our innocence at about three thousand years ago.

The primary problem was that humanity's awareness was blind-sided by sex, which had been around for a billion years. Our sense of truth attempted to confront it and lost.   How could we question something that had been around for a billion years? At that point, it all went to hell in a hand-basket (about the time of The Garden Of Eden).   Find someone to blame.   It ended up being women and a nebulous fallen angel.

I am sure there are those that will deny that Pandora and Eden had anything to do with sex. It's hard to deny the intent of the Kama Sutra. But, then again, some people really believe there was a snake and an apple and existence has only been around for six thousand years. Talk about deluding oneself.

This makes me think of my journey through these four books. It started with a lot of fury. It looks like it's going to end the same, though a different flavour of fury. I would never have gotten past all of the paradigms of nonsense without the initial fury of realization that I had been bamboozled by all of humanity's past. This later fury is directed at the stupour and has no respite other than humanity achieving clarity.

Much of the west and near east have been cowed into submission by some fictional god that will strike us all down if we dare think about sex. It's the way that god made it! So, just get used to it and all the misery it causes. Right.

Even more errantly amusing is the fact that the near east and the west (as well as smaller niches within the west) all praise the same god and, then, fight about it.

The funny thing about all of this is that many people realize that their gods are fictional and revel in the ability to use it to their advantage, which often involves very offensive behaviour. It seems, the opposite achieves the same results. Some conclude that since there is no god, thus there is no required responsibility for their actions. Like a petulant self-involved child. Who cares if one destroys the Earth. They'll be gone. Wanna guess what causes such bitterness?

The initial fury (that may never be completely gone) was required to burn through all of the nonsense that was inadvertently forced upon me over a lifetime. I was utterly outraged as I realized that the wool had been so thoroughly pulled over my eyes.

The nonsense that we accept on a daily basis as part and parcel of our existence in dystopia numbs us into acceptance *because* our awareness has been so dulled, dimmed, and intentionally distracted.

I find it even more fascinating that, as my outrage regarding our current state subsides, to some extent, in the wave of the certain realization that we can be so much more, the paradigms of nonsense fall away increasingly easily. The fury at our current state now just simmers. The helpless fury of attempting to purvey clarity has done a fine job of taking up the space.

Which makes me wonder even more about how a full-fledged race of sentient beings will react to patent nonsense. I'm no longer sure such foolishness will even be worthy of outrage. More exactly, as we become fully human, the outrage may be replaced with fierce clarity and intolerance rather than fury or amusement, as with the antics of a child.

Then again, sentient humans that live in a sentient existence amongst other sentient beings shouldn't expect to run into such absurdity very often. Surprise or pity may be the most appropriate feeling, but not tolerance.

The problem with the dreamer today is that it feels it needs to allow offensiveness to bash it over the head and just take it. That gives the offensively practical a huge advantage. Play by the rules versus break them to one's heart's content.

The point in the circle

Let us try looking at things from a different angle. What would be the responsibilities of the individual and humanity as a whole in a sentient society?

I don't think it will take a lot of training, whatever it ends up being. It just takes a dose of unadulterated self-respect. One thing for certain, it won't be "all about me".

Moral compass

During my earliest studies of what was wrong with mankind, as I've mentioned often, I studied religions, institutions, cultures, etc. All have effects on our moral compass and, yet, they do not override our *internal* compass or lack thereof. The best outside forces can do is a nudge in the right direction.

A moral compass suggests an internal guidance system. The best we have come up with is externally applied guidance systems: religions, cultures, and, inadvertently, institutions. So, we act is if there were no internal guidance system that we can rely on. It's not that it doesn't exist. It is just that it has been thoroughly undermined from birth in all of us.

What is even scarier is the thought that our external moral compass, which is about all we have so far, seems to be getting closer and closer to accepting morals as insignificant and only for fools. This is all due to the fact that we attempt to rely on outside influences to determine our behaviour.

The religions that sustained humanity for centuries are falling by the wayside as we outgrow their fiction. Our increasing sentient awareness is becoming uncomfortable with the increasingly obvious false premises on which they are built. There is little left to support our sense that morals are important - other than ourselves. We have mostly replaced our somewhat mystical religious externally applied moral compass with externally applied laws.

Of course, the rule of law is distorted out of any recognition of moral values by the influence of money and the foolish thought of "getting ahead", which only applies to animals. As the divisive wedge of factions is driven deeper and deeper, the whole process of law falls apart completely, as it is doing today. It becomes more and more the vehicle of the obsessively wealthy to swing things in their direction.

We are, at heart, seekers of truth. As something rings false, it irritates us and we seek to find out what it is exactly that rings false, unless one has fallen completely into depravity. The unfortunate inertia of the animal has misled us down a lot of crazy paths, none of them the truth. All because we mistook the animal's version of coitus as something that a human should tolerate. A large part of that was due to our ancient ancestors' inability to conceive of a way to make it human.

The internal moral compass provided by self-respect as well as confidence in self and humanity, and powered by the search for clarity and truth will straighten that all out in a hurry.

Our moral compass suffers because we have never realized that we do have an internal guidance system. No instructions required, just retention of self-respect.

Any outside force, such as the influences of moral fortitude provided by religions, or undermined by the corporate environment's inducement to "get ahead" no matter who suffers, or culture's peer pressure to "fit in", have only the slightest effect on who we are in this confused state of existence somewhere between an animal and a human. They should have no influence at all. They are but a distraction.

The long view

Trying to illustrate how this mosaic I am attempting to portray ties into the long view of one thousand years is straightforward. It is a matter of setting the groundwork infrastructure for attempting a most difficult scenario. It is a matter of attempting to crack open and explore a very complex gordian knot.

Okay, it's just hesitation and uncertainty as to the long view.

I think I may have found a way in which to circumvent the problem. Peer *from* the future. Sounds crazy, right? You might be right but some insights are sure to make themselves evident.

Infrastructure

The most significant change, in the final state, will, of course, be to humanity itself and the two genders and their interaction, less so the female gender since they already retain their sentience to some extent. That is the point.

We have never addressed what it means to *be* human. We just jotted down a lot of laws that may or may not make sense and then mangle them over time. We have just accepted what was handed down to us from the previous generation without question. 'Refining' the nonsense ad nauseam.

So, let's inspect the situation in which our humanity is whole. We will accept only truth and clarity without hesitation and continue to inspect anything that smells of nonsense. Our guiding momentum is provided by self-respect and confidence. Our morals will have their own internal guidance system, unencumbered by deceits embedded from birth. Our thought processes will work as intended.

It's pretty clear that some definitions of femininity and, especially, masculinity will change significantly. Some characteristics of the female gender will finally be accepted as human characteristics rather than just feminine. Like gentleness, understanding, stable emotions, maturity, sensitivity, openness, and willingness to let others in. I think it's safe to say those are *all* characteristics that will be common among *all* humans. They are not feminine. They are human.

Toxic masculinity will be a thing of the past. It's really difficult to describe any new, uniquely masculine characteristics that will become common to men to any level of detail, though I've mentioned a couple that seem more than likely. Forethought and discipline.

Real self-respect will make an end of the mess that is considered by many to be the quintessence of manliness. More so, toxic masculinity will be clearly seen as buffoonery and will quickly become completely relegated to the past.

Of course, the biggest question I have regarding the future is when do we *start* fulfilling our humanity? Today or a thousand years from now? It is beginning to press on my mind that most everyone seems to be willing to not take up the cry for resolution of our humanity but, rather, sit back and see what happens. Wow, is that just crazy? But, I guess, not unexpected.

Maybe we will remain stupoured.

History

I mentioned before that I can imagine our descendants pondering the state of their ancestors' conditions in horror. I think that was a mistake that gives me another a foothold regarding the future conditions as we fulfill our human nature.

Our emotionally stable, self-confident, and self-respecting, rational descendants will probably be more likely to view our current conditions and dilemmas as we view Neanderthals, Cro-Magnon, and Denisovans or even apes. They will only be viewed as some curious animals that preceded humanity. This is an evolutionary step of more significance than ever before, even though it does not involve genes. It involves becoming human by using the power of sentient thought to seek clarity.

They will view us and our current human condition as just another lower order of animal. They won't be wrong. This makes sense because it *is* evolution. It is a currently unexpected type of evolution, but evolution all the same. Cognitive?

After all, it will just be history to them that has little to do with a developed sentient state of existence. We don't become appalled by the conditions of our predecessors. We just accept their state. It's not ours.

A stunning difference is that they will be able to study the insane conditions much more closely than any previous exploration of history due to the mass of written history, documents, whimsy, and self-absorbed utterances that they will be able to access and pick apart.

We will only become completely appalled by our own conditions at the point at which we finally begin to acknowledge what it means to be human. The past will look very much like someone running in circles with one foot nailed to the floor.

Glimpses

I finally feel like I'm getting a glimpse into what it will mean to be human, loving, and sentient. That's nice, since I won't be around to see it happen. This may be the tip of the foil for which I've been looking.

I guess that explains nothing. How to explain? My very confusing childhood brought me up in the strangest way. I learned to love and adore women in tandem with the increasingly evident failure at coitus which burrowed into my mind rather quickly. Coitus was definitely where it's at. There were no other options for me. And, yet, I couldn't think about it.

But, loving a woman turned into something that I feared (subconsciously, of course) as well as cherished (consciously, of course). It was like this constant push and pull. The desire for sexual release was easily remedied. The desire for a woman's touch, not so much. I suffered because I would not compromise even though everything said 'just get used to it'. That's *really* not my style. I was miserable.

Now, I can think of a woman and imagine just how glorious it would be to *love* her *physically*. Not just have sex with her, not just satisfy my physical desires. Not just act like a loving being, putting on airs in order to cover up my failure at coitus and my failure to love a woman physically. But, create a loving fulfillment in the physical plane that easily expands into all of the planes of one's existence. Love a woman physically, emotionally, and expansively. That would be nice.

It is also no longer a deceptive desire. As my confidence builds, the desperation to find a woman that will tolerate the failure disappears. That changes the image wholly.

I'm not sure that conveyed what I hope but maybe someone else can make something of it.

The epitome of human

Authority

You may be familiar with the psychological experiments, knowns as the Milgram experiments from Yale University, that were performed regarding humanity's reliance (or dependence) on authority figures. There are two revealing aspects of the experiments in the context of our humanity.

To summarize briefly, the participants were told that they had to electrocute a subject sitting in a nearby room with increasing electrical intensity if the subject answered a question wrong (the subject wasn't actually electrocuted, they just played the part).

The conductor of the experiment, the 'authority' figure, would tell the participant to continue to apply electricity to the subject. The participant would often continue to apply the electricity, even after the one being questioned seemed to have died (or, at least, quit responding after screaming their heads off) because the authority figure told them to do so. I would bet many loved it. About 65% of the people were willing to kill someone because authority told them to.

In a world in which someone doesn't trust their own judgement, in which one's own confidence and respect is so thoroughly diminished, this is not a surprising outcome. It emphasizes that we have remained no more than Pavlov's Dog. We are *trained* to *act* human, but it remains only an act.

Let someone else make all the decisions, then you are only responsible for responding in the manner laid out for you. You can then complain about it later. We are still far from anything that resembles a sentient approach to life.

We can't trust our own judgement because we are living a lie and are utterly distracted by all of the fallout of allowing an important aspect of our animal legacy to remain in place.

Most of Pavlov's Dogs tend to follow some fool that claims himself a leader. It gives comfort to think that the loud, pompous, seemingly sophisticated, seemingly confident fool has the answers we so desperately desire. It's all a confidence game. Those are the ones that will electrocute until dead.

The simple, mangled, garbled answers are, of course, what only a simple animal would accept. They are answers for a trained dog. Those trained responses keep a person from ever asking, "What the hell?"

Anything more passes way over the bowed and trained dog's head. With the loud vociferous pontifications of the 'leader', we wash our hands of the absurdity. Someone else is taking care of it. Right. And such a good job, also.

More importantly, for purposes of where life might lead us once we undo the absurdity, once humanity has complete confidence in itself because it is not filled with falsehoods, authority will be questioned without the slightest hesitation. More exactly, our sense of truth, will throw out perceived nonsense, and offensive 'leaders' without a second thought.

Maybe, at some point, we will question the need for authority of any kind. Maybe a true indicator of humanity fulfilling its sentient state is that there is no one left that desires to be a leader (other than their own lives) and, more importantly, no one left that desires to be led like a dog.

This does not mean I condone anarchy, though I'm not sure it would be that much different than what we have. Dystopia by any other name. It all kinda looks like anarchy to me. It just waxes and wanes as we reach for our sentience once again and, then, dive back into the comfort of being only an animal.

There's only one way out of the maze. True independence and unobstructed sentience is attained by *learning* love in all of its endless, kaleidoscopic forms. It all begins with the physical act of loving.

Sandbox

I just had the oddest thought that I feel fits right in here. I am inserting it here since rereading and editing the previous paragraphs brought it on. Wow! This is big.

As I look back at others that have tried to change the world for the better, I realize that those that were best accepted were immediately proclaimed gods or god's messengers due to somebody's machinations. It's kinda funny, really, from a couple of standpoints.

One is that we can't seem to believe that another human, for all intents and purposes just like any other human, could make such a breakthrough.

I kinda envy Einstein. He could always point to the math. "It's not me! It's the math!" It kinda reminds me of Seldon. But, no, there is more to this universe than math.

Isn't it funny that we rely so little on our own human guidance that we can't trust new guidance from another human. It befuddles us. It is much easier to nod our heads to the guy that confirms all of the nonsense.

Gosh, this makes me want to get into the whole issue of the increasingly warped influence of cultural mores. Nowadays, the manipulation comes from advertisers and wealthy folks with an agenda. But, nah, 'nuff said on that.

The other funny thing this makes me want to suggest is that, somehow, we are offended to think that we are god. Not 'god' in any mysterious sense, just responsible for our own existence. It scares us spit-less. It is just so interesting that we have *always* chosen *anthropomorphic* vestments for gods.

We know we are responsible for our own fate, we just don't want to admit it. We want some daddy figure (what an incredibly bad idea that was) to lead us by the nose.

Whether we like it or not, we are masters of our own fate as a sentient race. Maybe it was just too big for our ancient ancestors to accept, right along with their inability to accept that coitus can be more than rutting. Blame it on some god.

So, yeah, we are masters of our own fate, whether we like it or not, and we wield massive power over everything within our purview. Scary thought that. I can see why our ancient ancestors ran from the thought.

We have attempted to avoid wearing the mantle of our humanity. We have hesitated for millennia. That's why monarchies made so much sense. There was something about that whole age of chivalry, royalty. It was short of the mark in so many ways but, in many of our first renditions of government, we were looking for something more and the only way we could accept the situation was to godify the rulers (sorry for the made-up word, but I don't think sanctify or any other word will do).

wowWoWWOW! I've been trying to pin that damned dot in place for ages. Wow! That's big!

There are a *lot* of dots that are connecting, right now.

We couldn't trust ourselves with big decisions so, like scared little children, we wanted to run to a ruinously godly Daddy.

Unfortunately, that was still just a human spouting nonsense.

We couldn't accept that we could be human, so we give someone else (that looks (and acts) just like us) the power to rule over us. We force godhood upon them. Wow. That's messed up, isn't it? The one good thing monarchies always had going for them is that there was always an attempt to train the rulers to act civilized. Most of the baboons running the show today have no such training and it shows.

We have such little confidence in ourselves, that we created gods to keep us in line and give us directions. Which ends up really being some fool human putting on airs in order to take advantage of the situation. Wow! I can't believe how fouled up that is.

We no longer need rely on fiction in our attempts to get beyond the radical change in life form from limited animal to sentient human. We are on the verge. We just have to try a little bit more in order to succeed.

As we become loving, we become sentient and, for me, that's a lot closer to something that I could accept as a god rather than the ruthless, obnoxious, self-involved creatures that we have *always* portrayed as gods. I am coming closer and closer to equating the two, sentience and loving.

The poor saps that take on leadership roles without the slightest clue regarding what is really being asked of them or willing to take advantage of the situation with no regard for the damage done. Sorry, dude, but them there shoes are bigger than any animal can wear.

Face the fact, folks, we *are* rulers of our own fate, each and everyone of us, whether we like it or not. We just have not had the wherewithal because we were lying to ourselves. It cannot be handed off to some god or some leader. That just exacerbates the problem. Only becoming fully, lovingly human will let us live sanely with the realization that we rule ourselves. Not some leader, not some god but each and everyone of us must lead their own lives in a sentient manner or we fail as a race. There is only one way we attain that state.

It's funny, the closer I come to full awareness of something sentient, the easier it becomes to see both the conservative and the liberal points of view and ascertain which of all of the polarized nonsense of either side is the valid underlying concept from which the nonsense is built. It usually involves both viewpoints. The split personality of humanity is further revealed.

Passion

Sentience is not a dispassionate existence. It is not an existence in which emotions should be locked away because they are in serious upheaval from about the time of puberty (or earlier). They are locked away or burst out in upheaval as we cross puberty because our sentience is not fulfilled but confounded. *That* is the only reason.

The journey *should* be filled with passion, exuberance, confidence, respect, joy, and love. All of the other perceived potential finer human qualities, like honour, integrity, etc are our natural vestments as a sentient being. They are only foreign to the animal we have yet to supersede. It all confounds the animal. The animal remains uncomfortable in human clothing.

We have never felt comfortable in sentient vestments. They don't seem to fit because we are only trained into them. There is no striving for these qualities. They either carry on and develop from birth or slowly erode.

That does not mean that there won't be challenges. It just won't be the fumbling, awful challenges created by the animal. It is not utopia but it is much less of a dystopia once humanity comes into balance with its sentience.

The problem isn't the presence of emotions. The problem is distorted, uncontrolled, unstable emotions that have no foundation from which to grow and no relationship to a sentient reality. They are undermined by pubescent failure.

Instead of puberty being a time of awkwardness and dissolution, it should be a time in which our sentience is confirmed and begins to become established (i.e. maturity).

It is like our humanity has been kicked out from under us since the beginning.

In many ways, we might think of our past as similar to a child playing in a sandbox. Just like children, we were impeded by lack of awareness of what is really going on around us. We exhibit temper tantrums as a race, just as a child would.

Unlike today, earliest humanity had no massive inertia of insane paradigms driving us. We invented them all along the way. The bewilderment caused by unfulfilling coitus misled us during our adolescence as a sentient race.

Just like a child, we still don't really want to take responsibility for our actions. It is time to face up to those actions. Especially rutting, loveless coitus. We'd rather blame it on someone or something else, because that is what we have always always done. How comforting to have some god or leader to blame it all on. "He made us that way. Woe is me." "We are only human."

We can no longer lay the responsibility at anyone's door but our own.

Human potential and liberation

What really stumps me on envisioning a sentient future is what an individual and the race will have the potential to accomplish once all of humanity is sane and our befuddlement dissipates.

I believe it will exceed my wildest expectations. And, if you haven't guessed, my expectations are anything but constrained. Certainly, that desperate desire for things to get better *after* we die should be long gone.

While I have said it is all about clarity, I'll go further. The pursuit of clarity will exceed all expectations.

The old saying that a person that has lived a full life can lay down his head peacefully comes to mind. Feeling fulfilled by this life can be true for the vast majority of humanity. There's only one thing missing and it is missing for most everybody.

The stability provided by the sentient fulfillment of loving coitus should eliminate the anguish that we regularly endure.

It is the answer to that vague desire for liberation that we have always sought. It is liberation from the animal.

Existence

The philosophy of existentialism as a description of our existence in this universe really makes me sad. It is so fouled up and hopeless that it leaves me in disgust. It explains everything regarding an animal to an animal.

There is just so much natural beauty in this universe (and, yes, enough chaos, also) that needs to be appreciated by a sentiently aware race. But, we can't see past our own problem (note: 'problem' is purposely not plural).

The idea that there is something in this universe that appreciates existence is gaining strength in me. It's not due to some gloating god. No, it is something much more subtle. Maybe humanity can figure it out once we gain our sanity and no longer hide behind a curtain of nonsense. Clarity.

If anything, that gloating, ruthless god is reflective of our animal state.

As the churning sea of insanity subsides, we will be able to look at the real situation of existence in this universe with clarity and address it properly.

Making the leap

A sane, fully functioning, emotionally stable, sentient human race one thousand years in the future. What would it act like?

For starters, it would be a race of individuals that do not contend with each other, but work with each other.

It would *not* be full of confrontation. In fact, I wouldn't be surprised if confrontation becomes virtually non-existent. That may sound like a stretch but think about it. What in the world does a sane race have to be confrontational about? It adds nothing. It smells of Asimov's quote.

It seems impossible for humanity to gain its sanity without attaining peace. Peace should not be a distant dream that only beauty queens invoke and arms are used in the attempt to assure. It should be part and parcel of being truly sentient.

I just have to make a side note regarding the whole contentious way in which we live. Does it make any sense to you? As an animal, sure, butting horns and acting superior seems natural. But, for a sentient loving race? It's really rather disgusting, don't you think? It's really insane. Can you not now trace its source? All the divisions of humanity make no sense at all. Does that help highlight the flaw in our existence? Can you see where I'm going?

Conclusions ... or not

It seems I have not provided a thorough contemplation of what the future for an emotionally stable, rational, confident, open-minded race that respects itself might entail. Or, did I? Do those adjectives not provide the vision? Are you still wallowing in nonsense? It is *not* about any change in anything *surrounding* humanity. It is about a change *in* humanity.

Okay, let me try, again, to make that leap ahead a thousand years and try to suggest what might be. As crazy as it seems, it might provide some insight.

One fundamental factor would be a race in which there are no hidden agendas because there is no deceit and nothing to hide, thus also no confusion about interests or positions. Informed and forthright innocence without the need for armour. Do you yet see how all of the deceit stems from one deceit?

I always feel that the hardest to swallow is the idea that deceit need not exist. It is so much a part of our lives today that I expect most will consider its absence preposterous.

We'll see. I think our honesty is one of the first and most crucial steps that comes from attaining our sanity. Don't think of it as a goal. That is the foolish way in which we have always attempted to achieve something more than our rough state. Think of it as a result of no longer requiring deceit in order to hide from all humanity the most ludicrous secret ever invented. Where do you think all of that pent-up hostility comes from?

A race within which everyone benefits. A race that fully believes in *stable* progress constrained by *rational* restraints that are easily accepted because they are sane.

Just keep in mind, our sanity is not a goal. Sanity is the result of admitting everything honestly to ourselves. It is a state of informed innocence and clarity.

Here's a prediction for you. I have always been seeking the ultimate high. I have found it: my humanity. While it is still tarnished by a life as an animal, it seems clear that there will no longer be a desire to escape the human condition through attaining "highs" in any form.

Everything else

Even deep in the environs of our inadvertently enforced idiocy, this life is just so astonishing that I can't get over it.

I mean, reveling in this life is an easy thing to do. Maybe that is why I was always so astounded by our enforced absurd, existential perspective. It is but a distraction from the amazing existence we inhabit.

Don't get me wrong, I can sympathize with anyone that throws up the white flag in surrender under current conditions. The current human condition ensures a lot of disheartening reactions that can easily place a person into a position of despair or acceptance of misery. I just couldn't ever give in. I guess, my circumstances were unique. I learned to avoid nonsensical situations like the plague.

Walking away from all intimacy with humanity is not an easy thing to do. It takes training from childhood to stand aside, watch it all happen, and finally see the joker in the deck. It really was like, "I'm not playing that stupid game. I am not going to prance across the Stage of the Absurd."

It's not pretty. It's not fun. I would not recommend it to anyone but, in this unusual case, it worked. For humanity, not me. The goal is that no one else is ever put in that position because the stupidity of the animal is gone.

Wrong lesson

What has become clearer and clearer to me is that, over the last few millennia, we have done nothing more than learn all the wrong lessons. We have been learning to be hopeless and feel helpless. Or its counterpart, a bluffing, false confidence that destroys all in its path.

Convincing oneself that everything one has encountered is all built on a single lie is challenging indeed. Bashing through all of the fear-inducing whispers that one should be struck by lightning for even having such thoughts takes a level of certainty (and no lightning arriving). The ideas of hubris, heresy, and betrayal all raised their ugly heads.

We've gone through a slow, brutal process of convincing ourselves that humanity is nothing more than an animal. The whole human narrative was set askew from the beginning.

It has slowly whittled away our confidence as a race. As we continued to fail to overcome our bestial instincts, we slowly succumbed to the conclusion that we must be just another animal with the rules of the jungle still in play or that god had cursed us into making this existence into a living hell. The "animal spirit" of Wall Street reigns more and more. "It's all about me." Gag.

Every time we have tried to be something more, we have slapped ourselves down in dismay and chagrin. All because we would not look in the mirror and admit what has never worked the way it should.

Redirect

After four books, I keep trying to find some way to get through to you. I realize the comprehension is startling but, still, it shouldn't be as difficult as it seems to be.

Maybe I'm minimizing how difficult it was for me to accept all of this. I have high hopes for this book, though. Maybe my broad brushstrokes of optimism were too much for most. That's the reason for this last book.

I still feel like maybe I'm not making it clear enough, even for someone with all of their wits in tact. So, I kept trying.

Let's try a few "elevator speeches". I'll make them more like a "going through a door speech" when possible.

- Men cannot love until they learn to make love. They cannot learn to *make* love until they can last indefinitely. Until we make unassisted coitus into everything it is advertised to be, we are lost.

Okay, that's the speech. Now, let me try to counter some arguments that aren't based on god or accepting the witless rules of the jungle that every animal before us has endured.

Some will say, "but we reach satisfaction in other ways." Doesn't count until the man is certain that he can do that which any human *should* be able to do: last as long as she pleases at coitus. It's a matter of the sentient awareness that it should be able to be done. It remains a failure and so do we. We were built for coitus. Why would humanity ever give up on making it human? It is cowardice to turn our backs on it and give up, which is exactly what we have done, so far.

Coitus is always advertised (by that I mean fictional representations) as most often being fulfilling for both. The studies prove otherwise. It is the biggest scam ever pulled and initiated all of the confusion, as well as the rest of the scams by making scams a part of our lives in the first place.

If it were difficult, if someone had to study and exercise and go through all kinds of effort to last indefinitely at sex (think *Kama Sutra*), that would be one thing. Obviously. *Kama Sutra* has a rather small following and, yet, it still has a following because coitus is just that important. Still, if that were what it took to become human, it seems a small price to pay. Thankfully, it is not.

Sexual competency of the male is similar to learning to walk or talk like a human. If you still don't believe that you can last, have you tried what I suggested? I don't think immediate success should be expected, just as you don't expect a child to be perfect at riding a bike or walking the first time. But, immediate improvement to some extent, especially if you pay attention, and go slow initially while you are learning, should give some confidence to continue a little longer.

It will take longer for men to learn the emotional aspects of love. The emotional stabilization and first glimpses of confidence and self-respect, though, should eliminate the surliness quickly. Three generations will have men loving well.

Another snapshot speech:
-   Men take and women give. In other words, men remain a beast and women, very naturally, emerged into sentience and their humanity with hardly an effort. Sadly, then they encountered the debacle that men endure. They have excused it and accepted it for millennia. That very natural, very beautiful sentient essence has been under assault by men so that it is battered beyond belief but, still, on rare occasion shines through.

And, the followup: Personally, I am appalled at the lack of awareness of the breadth and depth of the offenses against women. That has been so undersold that even women seem to believe that it is a matter of individual instances rather than the horrible human condition at work.

Can you give some other reason that all of the various faces of misogyny have existed for millennia? been shrugged off for millennia? Women don't even seem to be able to express how offensive it all is. Men, of course, seem witless regarding the situation. The scope of the atrocity is missing in all ways.

It has taken humanity more than three millennia just to accept that the offensive behaviour towards women is atrocious. We still don't seem to accept that it is pervasive.

The real question is why are men so atrocious to women? Why does inequity even exist? I hope, by now, that the answer is obvious. If not, then I really have been wasting my time. It is the essence of our problem.

What is really striking is that women should be the ones that are upset rather than men going berserk. (hint: giving is much more essential to attaining sentience than taking)

What also might be missing is the realization that loving coitus is like no other experience. Maybe what is missing is the comprehension by women regarding what it means, how it feels, to be the cause of such a momentous failure. The failure is not theirs, so all they see is the offensive results of the failure and never consider the failure itself nor its effects.

Many women seem to believe that men are happy with only their own release. Are you kidding me? Most men just have had no other choice up until now.

We are not sentient yet. Lousy coitus is the cause. We have to face that fact and address it. I have made the latter, addressing it, possible and easily so. The awkward way we dance around the subject destroys our sentient perspective.

Think about the facade that men erect (the pun is questionable). Men *act* as if they just don't care. That is only men's coverup for such a singular, unavoidable (until now) failure. It is like a child looking anywhere but at the window he broke. Some of the variance in coping with the failure may have to do with how severe the failure is. Maybe it takes longer for the failure to sink in for a man that lasts a few minutes. Being told "officially" that two minutes is success doesn't help.

Can you just imagine when no man disappoints a woman during coitus? Wow, that's big to imagine. At this point, I really have to wonder if there are any men that can say they consistently last until the loving is over. Maybe. If so, I'm not so impressed with your inability to think past your own success, figure out what it is that you do, and pass it on. You are still an animal because you think it is all about you.

All of the quirkiness, brutality, and beastly behaviours of a man are due to their broken manhood. All of the toxic characteristics of men can be attributed to the failure of loving coitus. A man cannot feel like a man until he can put the animal behind him in a big way. Men have to learn to give and it begins in bed.

And, a few more elevator speeches, without clarification:

-Most believe that human emotional stability is incongruous, impossible. Our emotional upheaval is just accepted. I'm not sure why that's true. Maybe many think the emotional vacuum of Mr. Spock or an automaton is an answer. It is not.

- Maybe another way to look at man's dilemma is in terms of the partnership that should be expected between man and woman. Each should pull their own weight, right? The man is at a disadvantage from the get-go. How can a man feel like he is pulling his weight when he can't even produce the coital results that a man should and does expect (whether we like it or not)? What a shock when it finally dawns on a man that it's all for naught. Equality and equity can only exist once men have nothing from which they hide.

- Maybe it would be different if there were really any difficulty in a man lasting long enough to love without assistance. But, there isn't any difficulty. Not for a human.

If there were then, sure, all of the antics, alternatives, aerobatics, and acrobatics, and means of assistance would make sense. Just as we have done since the beginning. It doesn't resolve anything but it makes sense in the absence of loving coitus. There can never be a substitute for loving coitus. The little blue pill is but a substitute for manhood. It resolves nothing and exacerbates the characteristics of failure.

- Think in terms of all of the traditions and rites of passage regarding men entering their manhood. It's really interesting. It is as if men have always known something was missing from their humanity. It is just another example of the bluff that men have embarrassingly and inadvertently been running for millennia. They are nothing more than a prop for a man's missing masculinity and damaged self-image. Poof! You're a man!
- I guess I just have such high expectations because I know what it would have meant to me to spend a life loving a woman thoroughly.
- Which leads to the final extrapolation. It's a guess, sure, but I feel rather certain that, once loving coitus is pervasive, a couple will easily last a lifetime. I'm not even going to explain.

Renewal

This final attainment of our humanity is all about renewal. Humanity completely renews its population after three generations or every one hundred years or so. A lot of momentum can be developed in one hundred years if the intent is purposeful, which it can be for the first time in history. No one should be puttering about once the realization sinks in.

It is not the millennia-long drudgery we have endured on the false hope of training Pavlov's Dog to behave.

The change will be grounds up. As more of us become human, all of the surface issues will become pliable because humans are now interacting as humans.

90%

Just like everyone else, I had about 90% of my brain contending with the absurdity of the human condition. The difference is that I was really focusing that small percentage of what wit was left on what was so fouled up for humanity.

That 90% will be a huge difference in a sentient humanity. All of the turmoil going on in our brains will be gone. We will be able to think clearly, precisely, and with purpose, once we are no longer contending with so many inconsistencies that are all due to our inhuman conditions.

Can you begin to comprehend how that comprises such a tremendous change? Can you conceive of what it will mean to put away all of those distractions? Our humanity and our brains continue to recede as women remain inequitably treated. How could we have ignored that for so long?

The barrage

The difficulty that humanity faces in realizing what is going on is becoming clearer. Whether we like it or not, our perceptions continue to grind away at what is inconsistent about our existence, even without my insights. Clarity is sought.

We are just so used to it all that we can't comprehend that it really can be different and that the difference is not where we supposed but hidden from us.

So, the momentum veers off in crazy directions because we have accepted that coitus is not fulfilling and never will be, we are animals and never can be anything more. We never even suspect the truth. Simultaneously, we seek fulfillment in aberrations instead.

For me, it was a huge leap to overcome the nonsense of the human condition. For you, it should be no more than a challenging exercise because of these insights you read.

The more influenced I become by our potential, the more aghast I become at the chaos of the current human condition in which I find myself. Not humanity, not humanity's potential, not human nature, just the appalling current human condition that is no more than the antics of a highly destructive animal that has not accepted its sentient awareness of what is really going on.

Some will fear that fulfillment. They will think that progress will just stop. That is just stupoured. I won't even bother to explain. There is a way out of all of the nonsense if we would just pay the slightest attention.

Before I realized this, it was easy to shrug it all off and think to myself, "What's to be done?" Just like everyone else, I would throw up my hands and think, "What is the *world* coming to?"

It's really fun to get all upset and angry until you realise it is all just the folly of the stupour. It is all just the existential view of an animal. Existentialism is just surrender to our animal legacy. It is purely bovine.

Initial conditions

Animals were having sex long before humanity came on the scene - by about a billion years. The transformative properties of sex that humans can reveal and fulfill were not a discontinuity that popped into being in a day. The initial condition was the sex we inherited from animals. Our ongoing, increasing awareness coupled with the desire for clarity was the new element. It created the slow realization, over the millennia, that there should be more.

Human comprehension of all of this was certainly not an initial condition. The first thoughts that stirred were closer to, "ugh, I'm hungry" and "ugh, I need shelter" and "ugh, I want sex." and not much else.

Maybe the next stage was, "Hmmm, women can get just as orgasmic as a man. Damn, if only I could last long enough. Why does she still act like she loves such as loser?"

That had to have happened a long time ago. The *Kama Sutra* dates it, even if you don't believe that the same subject is what Pandora's Box and The Garden Of Eden are all about.

They surely didn't have a good idea what to do about it, since here we sit three thousand years later with the same youthful sense that there is more to coitus which begins to get crushed out of existence as puberty takes hold.

Instead, we have just continued to find a way to make do. A thought that has always repelled me.

Now, it becomes clear that all of the befuddlement we have suffered, the misery we endure, that pall of sadness over our sentient state, are all due to this conflict between sentience and sex. The momentum has inexorably continued to delude and diminish humanity. We must find a way out.

Momentum

As the paranoia, confusion, dissatisfaction with life, and delusions begin to subside, a momentum of relief and joy will begin to build.

This will comprise a discontinuity. The animal's perceptions and delusions will be a thing of the past, displaced by reorienting our humanity to begin building a momentum of sentience. Split infinity. The animal finally becomes human in a virtual instant to split infinity forevermore.

The change in momentum to a human, sentient perspective should be stunning. I so wish I could see it as it happens. The change in momentum should encompass the joyful anticipation of what is to come as reality sets in, both in the individuals and the big picture.

The change I envision will not be a simple panorama. The emotional stability will begin leading almost immediately to a more sane perspective. Instead of change for change sake, a level of contentedness will seek change that makes real sense, that makes real change in the circumstances of humanity rather than celebrating any change which can be used as a distraction to dull the senses further. Personal responsibility and clarity will preside when self-respect and confidence remain in tact. So, I guess, I do explain why fulfillment is not the end.

Rules of the game

Once life existed, it became a matter of blind ambition, a blind desire to continue to exist under any conditions. Some make it and some don't. The rules of the game were set for an animal. Zero insight, zero imagination, and zero good will. A zero sum game.

With sentience, the rules of the game changed. We just never realized it.

The changing of the rules was not something we could do anything about. There is no avoiding our sentient senses that changed the rules. They predominate the new game. Only, our heightened senses remained obscured, distracted, deluded. Heightened awareness cannot be eliminated short of a lobotomy, but it can be obscured, derailed, confused, deceived.

Another description is that additional rules were added to the game of life for a sentient being. It has taken a very long time to suss those rules out.

Blind ambition is not enough for a human. Bind ambition, in fact, will certainly repel our unobstructed sentient perceptions. The blindness finally destroys a race that does not come to terms with its sentient awareness.

We continue to be pestered by legacy rules, like blind ambition, and bovine acceptance of circumstance, as the perceptiveness continues to grind away at what it is perceiving.

That perceptiveness has remained stumped on one particular insight. Coitus is not all it should be. It was stuck in the stunted rendition of an animal and no one admitted it.

Changing directions

Humanity, once we shed the blindness, will be looking towards the betterment of humanity and every aspect of our existence. It should be the mainstay for quite a few centuries.

Do you see where I'm heading with this? It will not happen in an instant but it will happen. We just need to finally open our eyes and look in the mirror without fear or quandary.

___Pure speculation___

As I reread and edit this book for the umpteenth time, I conclude that I am nearly finished. My fury regarding our past is beginning to dissipate. I truly hate how much fury was displayed in the previous books for the past acts of the animal. I do not despise the building fury of impatience to see it begin.

I am certain of the change and its importance to humanity. It's just the fine details of the future that remain vague.

In general, I think about all I can say with some certainty is that the dystopia that we endure, *the dystopia that we create*, will be gone. What will replace it remains to be seen.

The specific aspects of what humanity can be like without the burden it currently carries is really fascinating to contemplate for one that will not live to see it. The only thing certain is that we will be much more human and much less just an animal that has been driven insane by the conflict between sex and sentience once coitus becomes loving.

This will surely be the last book I write on the subject of attempting to enlighten humanity. I've finally written it in a form that anyone should be able to comprehend. I have also finally proven beyond the shadow of a doubt that any man can last indefinitely at coitus. It is now up to humanity.

If I see some glimmering of realization, I may go on to try to explain the changes to come better. We'll just have to see.

Summary

I've stated often that men need not fail at coitus and tried to explain *why* they need not fail at coitus. And, how men succeeding at loving, human coitus (as men have always believed they *should*) will transform the race.

Maybe there is another point to be pondered in that statement. It presents another of those odd facts that we ignore. Men are always trying to prove themselves. They are constantly trying to show how great they are. They try so hard to run faster, jump higher. Don't you find it odd that men have not found a way to last longer at coitus? They have treated it always as another case of running faster or jumping higher. No real thought was ever brought to the subject.

They haven't even really tried. They accepted failure and doomed the human race to millennia of Sturm and Drang.

Resolution

Men have been pulling an inadvertent bluff since the first day they realized that women could also have orgasm through coitus - and they had no idea what to do about it. Our existence has been a scam ever since.

The more I look around and observe, the more this insight explains everything quirky about the human race. All of humanity's offensive quirkiness can be laid at the door of this bluff, this deceit we have laid on ourselves.

The bluff blinds humanity to the problem that causes a sad state of existence in which humanity becomes more and more bamboozled.

It is an incredible pickle we find ourselves in. My previous books have caused people to accuse me of toxic masculinity. I now understand why. I'm awful fond of coitus, even though I have spent most of a lifetime being terribly bad at it. There are a lot of reasons for that fondness. It pretty much keeps the human race going, for one. The other primary reason is that I just adore women in every way. Now, I realize why. They have an underlying momentum of sentience that men cannot yet match.

So, imagine the frustration of a lifetime of the realization creeping up on me that I am about as bad as it gets at coitus. The bluff was the only reason for this.

Once a person begins to realize the situation, after being fed nonsense from their parents all during their developmental years, they tend to go haywire. The number of reactions are countless but they are all wrong. A man loving a woman should be as easy as breathing.

I could say that I have solved all of the problems regarding men and coitus (or ejaculation, if you prefer), but I am certain there is more to learn. Considering the feeble (essentially non-existent) efforts of humanity to resolve this (as well as ever look in the metaphorical mirror), I hate to leave the problem in the hands of anyone else. So, I have been driving myself to distraction trying to resolve the riddle of indefinitely delayed ejaculation thoroughly and decisively. That I have done.

I think I'm pretty much done. If humanity can't get it through their thick head that men have been running a bluff and, then take the next step and resolve the issue thoroughly for all men, it's not on me. I've done my part.

Just admitting the situation in which we find ourselves, is a big step forward. Otherwise, we remain a deluded animal.

It is not a lot to ask that all of humanity recognize the dilemma and, at least, admit there is a problem that requires resolution. I will balk until the day I die at the idea that anything can substitute for loving coitus. Even cunnilingus is but a substitute and does not fulfill the human desire. It may continue for unknown reasons as might every other form of sex and sexual partnering. I couldn't say at all.

Women have always intuited love because they do not fail to love their partner physically. Men have not. Their sense of love has never had a chance to develop. The reason is so straightforward it is clear just how bamboozled we have been.

Breakthroughs

And, this brings me back to the quandary of why it has taken me so many books to provide some level of clarity. It makes sense, really. It is a completely new field that has never been explored. We have never, ever desired to look in the mirror. It is the field of study of a sentient existence and the sanity of the human race, not just individuals. I was struggling to express in words what I knew intuitively from a lifetime of cataloguing quirky behaviour, nonsensical paradigms, and historical upheaval. I kept pushing the pieces around until something clicked.

My ongoing difficulties with thoroughly understanding why men fail to last indefinitely is another big part of my overall hesitancy. I understood *how* to correct the failure before I published *Sentience*. It was *why* that stumped me for the longest time. That is now well in the past. Any man can last indefinitely with the slightest effort and a base of rather simple knowledge, patience, experience, discipline and, finally, love.

Now that I think about it, I am sure there will be thousands of books written explaining the subject before we are done. Hopefully, one of them gets through. And, yes, I would really like it if it were this book. ;~j

There's, of course, much more to loving than mutual pleasure. Mutual sexual pleasure and emotional fulfillment through the act of coitus are just the starting point.

But, it is the crucial starting point. Without it, the loving intentions of any man wither on the vine as their life progresses and their failure becomes more prominent in their minds (almost without variation, at a subconscious level).

Note that it is only the grown man's loving intentions that are suspect. Most young men really seek love only to have it dashed on the rocks of their failure at coitus. To me, that proves the case.

I've also attempted to explain why men never got good at coitus and gave a lot of reasons and evidence regarding the situation and its resolution. Hopefully, it is enough.

The landscape is changing rather rapidly of late. Women are becoming tired of throwing themselves at men only to realize (or finally admit) that men can't hold up their end of the bargain in any way. They are also beginning to tire of being viewed as a punching bag, as well. Our consciousness, our awareness, continues on its relentless, remorseless path, whether we like it or not.

Women are beginning to realize it is all a sham. They are beginning to be open about finding ways to be sexually satisfied without the fumbling awkward, and often brutal attempts of men. They are finally beginning to become intolerant of the brutish aspects of unfulfilled manhood. That does not really improve the situation. In fact, it is an alarming development, but completely understandable.

Unfortunately, without resolution, without complete sentient insight, the two genders will remain in armed camps. That is not a sentient solution. It is just further miscommunication because no one has been willing to admit or accept what is really wrong *because* the resolution has continued to remain missing.

I can't wait until the real character, the human representation, of manliness is finally revealed. Men's essential character, once revealed, once the awful toxic caricature is removed, should be a revelation all its own.

Attaining that step to finally realize our sentience (much better than just reading a book about it), that life need not be this absurd existence, that we are still only following the inertia provided by the original humans that were not much wiser or informed than a monkey, though maybe slightly better than a rock, is what my books have been all about.

I am becoming so certain things are going to change and soon. We have been aimed in this direction for a very long time. I am concerned, though, how it will change and how long it will take to get it right. The fuze continues to burn on our insanity.

If we don't face up to the facts soon and ensure resolution, the rift it could cause in the human race is unlike anything we have ever seen and we've seen enough already.

We know all about the brute. We need to perceive the dementedness that causes it to exist in a sentient race. We need to put the animal away. Not by shooting it between the eyes but by transforming it into a human.

If men are forced to defend their absurd, foolish, witless position, all will be lost. That is exactly the direction in which we have been headed all along.

Without clarification and wit, the human race is being torn apart. Heck it has been ongoing, really, since the beginning but it is nearing a peak, at a breakneck pace, where it could tear the very heart out of the human race.

You want something to vote for? How about voting for a sentient, coherent, emotionally balanced, reasoning, fulfilling existence without deceit, delusions, irrational contention and aggressiveness, and utter failure of the human race.

Thread of thought

I've had this thread of thought that seems a very promising lead, though I'm pretty certain it is not one that I can follow to its end or convey completely.

What is it about us that desires honesty, justice, and balance, clarity? It filters through everything we do.

Is it just a matter of our heightened awareness and intellect? I think so. We seek consistency between what we perceive and what we comprehend. At least, the human, sentient part of us does. The animal says, "perception is reality."

To me, it seems like the tidal wave of life that sweeps up all in its path and sends it out looking for clarity.

The need for aesthetic balance came long before the realization or *acceptance* that something should be done to achieve it. Where we really stumbled and fell flat on our faces was not admitting what was wrong and exploring what *could* be done about it. Instead, we surrendered and declared life absurd, existential.

And, while I have harped on existentialism, that is not entirely fair. A precise definition of existentialism is not so bad. It is all of the connotations that were heaped on it that are the real failure.

Coitus

We have yet to accept that something *can* be done about our situation, even if subconsciously we know that something is broken. We don't want to admit that something is wrong while we cringe in the dark during coitus and try to make the best of a horrible situation.

Otherwise, these books, that I know have been read by a number of folks, would be flying off the shelves, especially *Sentience*. It is very difficult to get up the nerve to say, "I can do better", because it is admitting that you are not doing very well in the first place and the fear remains, "What if it doesn't work?!?" Especially since every bit of information tells you it's not possible.

I know in my case, subconsciously, I was always aware of the failure from the first time I had sex. It shook me to my core. It sent me down a rabbit hole for decades.

I only recovered when I could consciously accept that something was wrong and that something should be done about it. Resolving was the icing on the cake.

The cake itself was realizing that we can finally become human in a way that no one has ever suspected.

Natural

In all of my attempts to uncover what is wrong with mankind and discourse with others on my findings and their reactions, I ran into one of the most deluded and bizarre but, maybe most common, reactions. "It's just not natural for men to be good at coitus." and, its counterpart, "Women are just not meant to have orgasms." Usually followed by the ludicrous statement that "God made us that way."

NO! We were made to consciously adjust our environment, unlike the animals before us that have always had to adjust *to* their environment. *They* were made to endure unfulfilling coitus. *We* were made to discover the inconsistency and do something about it. We have been stopped cold by men's inability to admit there was something wrong in their helpless fear that made them unwilling to even look for a solution with any vigour and confidence.

What is natural for a sentient creature? We sure haven't a clue and, instead, substitute what is natural for an animal, when necessary, while substituting human capabilities only when we succeed. *That* has been a disaster, especially in the case of coitus, which has led to all of our other disasters. Failed coitus led to every other deception. We cannot avoid knowing that women should be able to enjoy the pleasure of orgasm during coitus, if only the man could figure out how! That destroys us, especially if we don't acknowledge it.

That has caused us to put our intelligence on a pedestal and our emotions, potential for love, and finer qualities in the closet.

What is natural for a sentient creature is to apply its heightened awareness, intellect, creativity, and curiosity to provide clarity and resolve issues. If that were not true, we'd still be lurking in caves scratching our asses, crawling around on all four and saying, "Ugh!" alot.

What is unnatural is brainwashing ourselves into thinking everything is alright. What is unnatural is lying to ourselves about coitus and all aspects of sex.

This is real

It really is nice to be at this point finally. This is real. Whether anyone gets it is another matter but I have done all I can to move us forward. I can only lead the jackass to water. It is up to them to transform themselves into a human by drinking deeply from the Castalian Spring.

Inducements

Think of early man. He had a desperate desire for sex and every reason to justify having sex often, even though humanity's awareness, at some point long ago, caused men to realize that there was something wrong: men's inability to sexually satisfy a woman.

Even worse, the transcendent joy of orgasm, more than likely, threw every other thought out of his head, other than, "I want more of that!"

He was satisfied, so what's the problem? Can you see where that leads? He never let a little thing like the dissatisfaction of the woman impede his desires. Early man was not confounded by his lack. He just accepted it and relegated the woman to the second sex.

He manipulated everything in order to get sex often. In that effort to continue to have sex in the absence of a solution to making it last long enough to satisfy the woman lies all of our problems. He had to create a wall around the problem. It has taken us more than three thousand years to scale that wall.

Whether the man likes it or not, he learns selfishness in bed as long as he cannot satisfy the woman. He makes every effort to satisfy and fails spectacularly for a lifetime. How do you think that makes him feel? Look at old men in the news. That answers all questions. There are a few that I would particularly like to call out but there would be no point. Like me, they will be dead soon enough.

The herculean tolerance of women, over the ages, probably saved us from destruction but it could never end the fiasco. The end to the fiasco has, by necessity, always been required of men.

The slight effort required to learn to satisfy a woman in bed will be well compensated by our emerging humanity. Not to mention men being able to look at themselves in the mirror with confidence and respect.

The selfishness displayed by men is only due to this stealth conflict that has never seen the light of day. The selfishness is the result of the inadvertent and unnecessary justification of the failure that became second nature, thus abdicating resolution. The selfishness displaced self-respect and confidence in a man. Even openly accepted failure is better than what we have endured. But, loving coitus is the only complete resolution.

Early man was about as bright as a bag of rocks. *You* are a different matter indeed. What is your excuse?

Just because

What our sentient sexual dilemma comes down to is that *because* we know that coitus can be so much more, it *has* to become so much more. A sentient being is driven crazy by knowing something so essential can exist without ever achieving it. In other words, our sentience has always known better.

Worse yet, because we hid from the dilemma, it distorted everything regarding our existence as a sentient being that depends on coitus to continue to exist. It is a daily trial in which we continue to fail.

Just look around you at all of the hurdles that humanity has overcome. How do you think that failure to make coitus into something more (and turning out the lights) sits with such a self-aware race?

We scurry around and avoid the question, as well as the situation and results, like they don't exist. That's insane.

If it's broke

When it comes to coitus, it seems like a great portion of mankind lives by a derivative of the saying, "If it ain't broke, don't fix it."

"If it's broke and you can't figure out what's wrong, just ignore it, make it all go away. Squash any mention of that crazy idea. I mean, who ever heard!!! Act like everything is okay!" This has been our response to these troubles. Do you see its shadow across all of the nonsense we tolerate?

Most intriguing is that any mention of the idea that men can last indefinitely has been treated as foul or evil by some. It is just so crazy as to belie description and I am not going to take the time to ponder why this happens.

We should be ashamed. It goes back to that Japanese proverb.

A wall of untold proportions

Our less than human behaviours are *exactly* humanity's problem and *they are caused* by the lack of love that is due to the lack of human, sentient coitus that fulfills us enough so that we can fulfill love. That is especially true of the male of the species.

It still irks that some have responded with the suggestion that I am being toxically masculine with all of this. That blows my mind. Is it toxically masculine to want to love a woman? Is it toxically masculine for a man to desire to please a woman in bed? Is it toxically masculine to be crushed by the lack? I just don't get it. Is it offensive to want humanity to finally attain the human state that we have sought for so long?

Going at life like a witless, blinded bull will never get us there. Bull-headed acceptance of our situation and failure and an unfulfilled commitment to love is a travesty brought on by the absence of fulfilling, human, sentient, loving.

Maybe a better way to describe loving coitus may be coitus that fulfills us so thoroughly that we can become loving by achieving equity in the sexual situation leading to equity in every instance. Whatever.

There is so much more to humanity once we realize that we have been justifying something that deserves no justification. It needs reparation.

Words

What I really love about this is these written words are not at all important. It's not like someone will be reading these some hundreds of years from now, seeking some hidden, mysterious meaning.

These words become unimportant once the narrative of loving coitus becomes common. The real understanding will come from loving coitus. Once achieved, we will not regress. It will be intuitively obvious to coming generations. No words can replace the loving intimacy of coitus and its after-effects. It stands on its own, once achieved. Words are no longer needed.

Paradigms

I hope you realize, I was only one step ahead of you as I wrote these books. I was figuring it out as I went along (with virtually no help from anyone - that has been my life).

The initial insight struck like lightning. It would have been nice to have had a lifetime to ponder before publishing but my time is close enough to used up.

So, I felt it necessary to write as I learned. There was always the chance that someone was out there with an open mind and at least the words, the sketch of the concept, would be out there, even if I went kaput. That, by the way, would have saved me a lot of trouble (double entendre intentional).

There was no surety in the first words and version of *Sentience* (I have revised it many times since then). There were a lot of "it seems like" and "maybe", initially. There may still be a few. There may even be a few in this book as I finally grasped everything necessary to last indefinitely while this book was still in the works. I have eliminated any doubt from this book as best I could.

The explanation has been a long drawn out process with which I thought I would have been done long ago. I would have been more than happy to let others take up the torch. No one picked up the torch.

I did so many different things to try to figure out what everybody's thoughts on this subject were (those bizarre thoughts are the only help I ever received). Most important that

I have spent the last decade doing, was circumventing all of the nonsensical paradigms of my own.

Now, after multiple reviews and conversations, I have a much better sense of the disturbance ruling people's perspectives. They broke my heart but, more importantly, it breaks a person's ability to accept a sentient perspective. **_Everyone_** is too caught up in justifying their own stunted, stultifying compromises regarding life, sex and, particularly coitus.

It is not about what *you* had to do in order to sidestep the worst of the nonsense of our current human condition. It is about humanity overcoming the root cause of its insanity. It is about ridding humanity of the nonsense, once and for all. It is about ridding humanity of the misery it has learned to embrace like some victim of the Stockholm syndrome.

It's those frigging paradigms. I sympathize with all of those that had to make tough choices in order to move forward in life. But, you have no idea about tough choices until you face and attempt to elucidate all of the nonsense and its resolution, on your own, with zero support. The relief, for me, is saying those words without bitterness (but certainly still a touch of fury). If I can avoid that bitterness throughout what is left of this life, I will be well please. The chances of my own fulfillment in this life are minimal, at best.

The more I study our quirks the more I realize how much we act like a bunch of packs of animals vying for dominance, varying only in the version of insanity and the split personality that is supported. That is also replicated in the individual mentality. It truly and utterly disgusts me.

No one has been looking for resolution to the human condition. All are just trying to emphasize their own version of the lunatic human condition.

Everyone is attempting to carve out their own little niche amidst the insanity and to hell with everyone else. "It's all about me." Another phrase I utterly despise.

Just keep this in mind: we are talking about humanity finally turning the corner and becoming truly human. It's about coitus not being at all as it has been promoted (yet!).

We took the remains that the animals left us and rode it. All we need do is make coitus match what we so obviously desire to be the case: a loving, intimate engagement filled with mutual physical and emotional satisfaction and fulfillment.

It is *the* human issue that has yet to be addressed by humanity. It is a human versus animal issue, which has to do with the way coitus is perceived and executed. For an animal, it is just something that occurs with no intellect involved. *For a human*, the intellect *will* become involved, whether we like it or not. We attain our humanity by making coitus into a successful *human* endeavor. We can't hide from it, as much as we try.

We have no choice but to perceive coitus differently than the animals that came before us. So far, we have accepted it unchanged. We obliterated a sentient perspective of coitus.

Your little piece of an acceptable version of the nightmare that you have come to terms with is not good enough. Look around. They have all been tried and none have resolved our irrationality or made *the human race* human. Walling yourself up in your own delusions, or studying your navel, is not enough. The *human race* has to become human, not this or that individual. That never amounts to anything.

The realm of sentient humanity is far distant from that of an animal. Once we achieve our sentience in full about all we will have in common with other animals are some genes.

This is not about the individual repeating some mantra endlessly for a lifetime in order to stay sane. It is about all of humanity naturally staying sane without the slightest effort.

I have always worried about some nitpicking idiot perceiving that when I say something like "all of humanity", they can nitpick away. Yes, of course some people may still derail for a number of reasons, though it is not certain. There will certainly continue to be car accidents and natural phenomena that cannot be avoided.

We are not just an animal. Our current state is nothing more than a failed attempt by the human animal to achieve its inherent sentience. All we have done, so far, is mimic the gift and besmirch its magnificence.

Obsessions, aberrations, and 90%

We obsess about the small stuff because that which makes life make sense *for a human* has been withheld - by our own forced blindness. *Remove the blinders.* Get on with it.

The world that animals perceive makes sense to them. Our heightened awareness made gibberish out of an animal's perspective. We have struggled with that for millennia, always regressing to the animal's view.

We have known for a long time that there was something more to life than an animal perceives and we called it love. We just never connected the two most important, inextricably connected, dots for reasons explained throughout these books.

It ends up, as I look deeper into our insane conditions, that there has built up, over the millennia, so much that we don't want to admit. All because we misunderstood love and its source. Maybe a better word than 'source' is 'enabler'.

We all have biases built into our views that have nothing to do with reality. The biases are the ways in which we learned to justify (not just cope with) the insanity that we endure. We accept way too much as gospel, like a bovine animal.

Human life is way more complicated than it would be without all of the clutter of nonsense that is caused by not fulfilling our humanity (that wasted 90%).

I really wish I could find the complacency verbalized by Kimitake Hiraoka when he said, "even if I am not immediately understood, it's okay, because I'll be understood by the Japan of 50 or 100 years' time."

I guess the problem is that I feel my words could be lost in the torrent of words being thrown out by humanity daily, if I don't find a way to clarify and gain momentum before I die.

The best I can come up with as an alternative is to say that even if humanity doesn't get it, I've done my best and I fully understand, even if I can't convey it in a way that others can comprehend. At this point, the words are there. There is nothing to add. I have not been idle nor lacking. Still, the following words tastes like ashes. We will get there, sooner or later, if given enough time. Sigh.

Not all that satisfying but, there you go. We are generally headed in the right direction, though the detours are becoming ridiculous and there are dangerous curves ahead unless we see through the bullshit soon. I won't be around to see either result.

I also told myself that, now that I've come to terms with the real, sentient universe, I could coexist in both. After further thought, I am not so sure that is true. How do I relate to anyone that still accepts all of the lies, absurdity, and utter nonsense that humanity has told itself over the millennia without question? Whether they rail away at it all, accept it as fait accompli, accept the dark side as inevitable, or become bitter self-serving automatons, how can I possibly have any conversation of significance? I think I need another lifetime.

Hmmm, it seems I have been remiss in adding the ongoing list I have been compiling regarding the finer qualities that humanity has the potential to achieve, once it becomes human. So, here it is. I doubt it is complete. Maybe it can never be complete.

It starts with self-confidence and self-respect which engender, reinforce, and sustain self-worth, caring, compassion, empathy, generosity of spirit, honor, integrity, responsibility, civility, sensitivity, grace, joy, decency, honesty, innocence, and the celebration of life and existence in all of its aspects.

In the end, in the fullest state of our sentience, is love. None can flourish in the absence of self-respect. All of those human characteristics are all based on feelings of self-worth. It all falls apart as long as we rut like animals.

Magic

I now realize that this, the full ramifications of love and loving coitus, are the magic for which I have always been looking. I am in awe. It was always right there in front of me. May we all become wizards soon.

It is so interesting to me that, in my poetry that I wrote for someone over the last few years, I used the term wizards quite often. It highlights that intuition I find in poetry.

All of my life I have sought magic, never suspecting that I was using it to describe love and an unobstructed sentient existence.

The poetry

Innocence

In rage I sit brooding
Before life is past
Delusions occluding
The iconoclast
If faith is a must
Set your faith in your kind
Bring a bounty of trust
To all of mankind

Rather than bow
To the figment of priest
Release sacred cow
Love mankind, not the beast

The fury I feel
On this miserable day
The love that we steal
In that witless old way

Release now, from ancestors
Hidden in cave
From the blindness that festers
And learn to behave
Loving humanity
A full tidal wave
Of beauty and sanity
That all of us crave

Read through the dust
Of my ashes before
I rise in disgust
To this rubbish, once more

I ached for the love
of a woman renowned
But I could not behove
While humanity drowned

So, make of it certain
That, with the next round
That, at last, we uncurtain
At last, we astound

I learned so much in this lifetime that I have not mentioned that would astound you. Of course, if revealing the source of all love was not enough to astound you, then nothing would. Right?

Poetry from a very, very different book.

The Reason For Unreason
In the depths of distant time a sentience emerged
Onward, upward, was the passion that their essence urged
But, chaos did ensue for they had made a grave mistake
Embarrassed and unwitting, they had thrown at heart a stake
Love and honour were the ones that fell upon the ground
As witness to the sad affair, all reason was unsound
A pall occurred when mention of the act was ever made
So silence and unreason took the stage and farce was played
To see the truth and shout it, only echoes do return
Until the truth is evident for all, this heart will burn
Rage and fury settle in, for price that we have paid
A challenge made, a gauntlet thrown, that reason will cascade
I cannot seem to raise the tide, a glamour does reside
My will is not enough, it seems, to raise the ocean tide
But, will and effort integrate, an iron without match
A hammer built for all mankind to break unreason's hatch
Forged in our humanity, while flames were flying high
A breath of life for all of us, a message in a sigh
Life and living's hard enough without unreason's weight
Take the chance of life and heart and, then, you radiate

There is an answer to the drum that's heard on summit's peaks
A spinal fire that runs along undoes what havoc wreaks

Solo flight
I spread my wings as I fly all alone
I soar above the clouds all on my own
It is the only way this life could be
As I search on throughout eternity
To show the answer to the conundrum
The reason why mankind remains so numb
It's been a lonely flight along the way
But, celebrations still come every day
Five minutes has become five years, at least
To rend humanity from maw of beast
The simple-minded way in which we live
A barrier to burst, so on I give
Way more than I expected at the start
To free the love and open up the heart

Tides of confidence
As I stride the shores of life and doubt
Tides of confidence wash in and out
The slightest indecision genders bout
A flaw or imprecision renders rout
The ripples in the waves presage a storm
I look to sea to view its mass and form
But, in the depths is drawn from moon above
The surge of confidence in heart and love

Outta here

I noticed, when I was very young, as I sat in a bus station in Bangor, Maine, that *no one* present at the bus stop had any expectations of me. I was free. It was the most amazing feeling of revelation. I tried desperately, earlier in life, to surround myself with people that could accept me *as I wanted to be*, rather than that into which I had been molded.

In my old age, I have taken that to heart for ten years. It freed me from all expectations. It freed me to look at life through a telescope and under a microscope.

This final resolution over the last decade, in which no one had any expectations regarding my reactions to all of the foolishness, was crucial. It set me completely free from all of the ties to the nonsense from our past.

I did not have to act like any of the absurdity of the human condition was okay. No one was expecting it of me. I would not and will not accept any of the nonsense. Only its resolution.

Wow! Fifty years of a deep dive. Forty years, followed by a decade of some incredibly intense concentration to reveal why humanity remains such a mess. I could write on and on, I'm sure, but it's time for the intense concentration to end. It is time for, at least, some few to get a clue and carry on. If I sound annoyed and disgruntled, I am. There's a reason I use the image below. I'm done.

I now know we have the potential to become human soon, not in some distant, vague future. But, *__now__*.

You have to change the initial conditions. The most initial condition of all is sex.

It's about clarity.

I'm outta here.

W

Thank you for buying the book

whickwithy@gmail.com